Sotheby's
CAFE COOKBOOK

A CELEBRATION OF FOOD AND ART

featuring seasonal recipes by Laura Greenfield, Head Chef

CONTENTS
5

'One of the best lunches in the west end is to be
had at this interesting rendezvous, off the auction
house's foyer; it offers a short but imaginative
menu, great service and a relaxed style –
good people watching is thrown in free'

Harden's, 2005

'Short-notice reservations are hard enough to get anyway, so it's good news for Sotheby's Cafe regulars that more people don't know about it. Small, intimate and clubby, it's roped off from the foyer like the VIP area at a movie premiere. This is the chicest spot to lunch on Bond Street, and chef Laura Greenfield's seasonal weekly changing menu means you can eat here all the time without ever getting bored.'

Tatler Restaurant Guide, 2006

Adding a new, unexpected, dimension to the business, Sotheby's Cafe opened in New Bond Street in 1996. An unabated success for ten years, the origins of the Cafe, as so often with such endeavours, is rooted in the eye for detail and exceptional commitment of those who advocated establishing something unique in the auction world.

In order for Sotheby's Cafe to fit into that environment it was launched with – and has retained – a special charm, with time-lessly elegant dark wood, mirrors and brown leather banquettes and black and white prints from Sotheby's archive of Cecil Beaton photographs. The idea for a Cafe grew from the need to create an exclusive area to entertain clients during viewings and auctions, and the idea of making this into a commercial café was a stroke of genius. The reception area in New Bond Street was the obvious location for the Cafe, convenient for those attending auctions or simply passing by in what is one of London's most exclusive areas. Early in the process it became apparent that further seating would be required and, in occupying a greater area of the Bond Street entrance, Sotheby's Cafe acquired the feeling of a 'pavement café', where it is possible to see successful (and disappointed) bidders passing, gallery staff carrying works of art for clients or hanging the next exhibition – in short the hive of activity that is an auction house during sale season.

What really adds life to any establishment, of course, is the food, and Sotheby's Cafe has been known for both service and menu since its earliest days. The style of cuisine reflects the diversity and polish of the Cafe's clientele, and with a definitive 'lunch style' the food is adjusted to reflect not only the season for produce but also, to some extent, what is taking place in Sotheby's galleries in any given week. The recipes in this book are taken from the regular menu at Sotheby's Cafe and, ordered to follow the auction season from autumn to summer, they serve to show the range and inventiveness of the menu organised by head chef Laura Greenfield. Notes on wine accompany each season in this book from the head of Sotheby's Wine department, Serena Sutcliffe MW, a world-respected connoisseur. She has also been responsible for tailoring the wines at the Cafe to suit the menu and, under her inspired guidance, the succinct wine list has received outstanding reviews.

Combining the exceptional artworks sold by Sotheby's around the world with recipes from Laura, this cookbook, a celebration of ten years of success, is a testament to the vision of those who founded Sotheby's Cafe, which remains an integral part of this thriving business within the world's oldest fine art auction house.

Ken Hall, General Manager, Sotheby's Cafe

AUTUMN

Decorated with the natural shapes of corollas, palmettes, arabesques, lilies, insects and snails inlaid in coloured antique marble and hardstone, this table-top sold in London in 2000 for £1,136,500 ($1,655,260). This type of ornamental design has its origins in ancient Rome, and was employed in the city from the late 16th century, later flourishing in the Florentine Medici workshops throughout the 17th century

This delicious soup is a favourite with patrons during the Russian sales. Adding vinegar gives it a distinct sweet and sour flavour

BORSCHT WITH SOUR CREAM & DILL

Serves 6 • Preparation time: 1 hour • Cooking time: 10 minutes

1 carrot, peeled and finely chopped

1 leek, finely chopped

1 small onion, peeled and finely chopped

1 stick celery, finely chopped

450 g/ 1 lb/ 3³/₄ cups beetroot, peeled, cooked and roughly chopped

1.2 litres/ 2 pints/ 5 cups hot chicken stock (page 154)

1 dessert spoon caster sugar

4 dessert spoons red wine vinegar

To Serve

Sour cream

6 sprigs of dill

First prepare the chicken stock (page 154). Gently heat some olive oil in a saucepan, add all of the chopped vegetables apart from the beetroot and stir for 5–10 minutes until soft but not brown. Set aside half of the vegetables. Place the beetroot, the other half of the vegetables and a couple of ladles of chicken stock in a food processor and liquidize until smooth. Return to the saucepan, heat gently and add the remaining stock and chopped vegetables with the sugar and vinegar. Season to taste.

Drop a spoonful of sour cream and a sprig of dill onto each serving. This soup can also be served chilled.

The 'gamey' flavour and texture of venison is delicious and more distinctive than beef, which could be used as an alternative

SEARED VENISON

ROAST TOMATOES, BALSAMIC SYRUP & PARMESAN STRAWS

Serves 4 • Preparation time: 45 minutes • Cooking time: 15 minutes • Pre-heat oven to 220 ºC/ 425 ºF/ gas-mark 7

300 g/ 11 oz venison haunch or fillet

100 ml/ 4 fl oz/ ½ cup balsamic vinegar

225 g/ 8 oz plum or cherry vine tomatoes

To Serve

Parmesan Straws (page 156)

Sprigs of flat leaf parsley

Prepare the Parmesan straws first (page 156). Pour the vinegar into a pan, place over a high heat and bring to the boil, then reduce by three quarters and leave to cool.

Place the tomatoes on a baking tray, drizzle with olive oil and season. Cook in the oven for 6–8 minutes until they are soft but retain their shape.

Season the venison generously on all sides. Heat a little vegetable oil in a frying pan, then cook the meat in the pan until all sides, including the ends, are browned. Transfer the venison onto a baking tray and place in the oven for 3–5 minutes. Remove and allow to rest for 5 minutes before slicing.

Slice the venison thinly and fan around the edge of four plates. Place the tomatoes in the middle with the Parmesan straws on top. Drizzle a couple of teaspoons of balsamic syrup over the plates and decorate with a few sprigs of parsley.

The animal painted on this 14th-century Yuan Dynasty blue-and-white dish appears to be a deer, but is in fact a mythical creature known as a 'qilin' in Chinese, a good omen that brings prosperity. This dish sold for £473,000 ($785,180) in the Chinese Ceramics and Works of Art sale in London in 1987

These can be made a day in advance. When re-baked, the soufflés form a lovely golden crust while the centre remains soft and light

Twice-Baked Smoked Haddock Soufflé with Creamy Leek Sauce

Serves 6 • Preparation time: 50 minutes • Cooking time: 45 minutes • Pre-heat oven to 200 °C/ 400 °F/ gas-mark 6

Soufflés

Melted butter for lining 6 ramekins

*3 dessert spoons breadcrumbs
for lining ramekins*

500 ml/ 17 fl oz/ 2 cups milk

1 bay leaf

3 pinches of ground nutmeg

3 pinches of ground mace

1/2 tsp salt and ground black pepper each

*300 g/ 101/2 oz skinned, undyed
smoked haddock*

25 g/ 1 oz unsalted butter

40 g/ 11/2 oz/ 1/3 cup plain flour

1 heaped dessert spoon chopped dill

11/2 egg yolks

2 egg whites

Creamy Leek Sauce

(page 150)

Heat a large saucepan of water for the *bain-marie*. Next line the ramekins with melted butter, coat with the breadcrumbs and set aside.

Pour the milk into a saucepan and add the bay leaf, nutmeg, mace, salt and pepper, before adding the smoked haddock. Cover and bring to simmering point, then remove from the heat and leave for 5 minutes. Put the haddock on a plate to cool, strain the milk reserving 300 ml/ 1/2 pint/ 11/4 cups for the soufflés and the remainder for the leek sauce.

In another saucepan melt the butter then add the flour, gradually adding the milk reserved for the soufflés, stirring to avoid lumps. Boil the mixture for 1 minute and remove from the heat. Flake the haddock and discard any bones, then add it to the sauce with the dill and egg yolks and allow to cool for 5 minutes.

Whisk the egg whites and fold into the sauce with a large metal spoon. Divide the mixture between six ramekins and put in a deep oven tray, half-filled with boiling water.

Bake for 20–25 minutes until well-risen and golden brown on top, then take out of the *bain-marie* and leave to cool. While these are cooking, make the leek sauce (page 150). Run a knife around the edge of the mould and gently ease the soufflés out, cover and put them in the fridge.

Reheat the soufflés upside down on baking parchment for 10–13 minutes until they form a golden crust. Heat the creamy leek sauce and spoon onto the plate around the soufflés.

A Chef's Palette

Frans Snijders specialised in
painting animals, hunting scenes
and still lifes, often collaborating
with his close friend Sir Peter
Paul Rubens. This kitchen
still life, which sold in London
in December 2004 for £212,800
($389,275), from *circa* 1605
is a previously unknown work
by the artist

Ideas for recipes can come from many sources. Laura Greenfield, head chef at Sotheby's Café, and Jesse Dunford Wood, head chef of the National Dining Rooms at the National Gallery in London, seek inspiration from Frans Snijders rendering of a 17th-century Dutch kitchen and discuss the process of devising recipes.

Laura Greenfield: I started as a chef almost by accident, I went to drama school and, as a backup, did a cookery course and really loved it. Although I did bits of acting work, I ended up doing more cooking and eventually worked with a friend in a small restaurant and my career in cooking began from there. I think in some ways acting and cooking share a similar flamboyance – you build up to a performance, then it goes manic, and then you can relax after a great service.

Jesse Dunford Wood: All of my family are artists and I was destined for art college, but six months before I was offered a job in a restaurant and took to it. I love the science of cooking and the discipline and organisation of working in the kitchen. I am a fanatical organiser. Another element is the creative part and the sense of bringing people together. In addition to working as a chef I have worked as a waiter and you suddenly become part of the customer's experience, whereas in the kitchen, it is food in, food out. You sometimes have to tell people: 'remember, this is for someone who is going to have lunch'.

LG: I agree. That is so important to remember when all you get is a docket with an order. You have to be fast and you have to be right. Our menu changes frequently so it is easy to adapt food for clients coming into Sotheby's. There is a noticeable difference of people coming in during a week of Russian sales, than say a week of Old Master paintings auctions. So even though it is difficult to find the time to look around the galleries properly when we are busy the clientele are completely different and eat different foods.

JDW: We try to retain the same British menu as we are in such a British institution. I occasionally get to look around the National Gallery exhibitions, but we don't adapt the menu to reflect what the special exhibitions are. Really though when you are busy you could be anywhere. I worked in Australia at the Sydney Opera House and it was weird to be working against the clock in this enclosed space and look up and recognise the Sydney skyline.

LG: I do try to keep the menu seasonal as well as taking some inspiration for menus from the auction calendar. In summer for instance people want light stuff, and other than that I do I want, bearing in mind that we have many regulars who come to the café on a regular basis. I also work really closely with our general manager Ken Hall to get feedback on dishes. We do have certain limitations though, so rather than cooking a large side of lamb like that shown in the painting we would take single portion sized pieces as we have to work within certain margins. Often the commercial concerns of the café take over from the direct inspiration for menus.

JDW: I read a lot, I take ideas from eating out, I look a lot, I take inspiration from other recipes – no one is stealing, lots of dishes are versions of other things.

LG: Obviously you can't plagiarise, but people adapt and change recipes all the time, from a cookbook, from a friend. They become a guideline and I rarely follow them to the letter. The recipes I have put together in this book are the product of a lot of development. We serve all of them in Sotheby's Cafe and each time they appear on the menu I will find a different approach to creating them.

JDW: I think you also take inspiration from your career, from where you have worked. I started cooking in Scotland, then went to a serious French restaurant in Devon, then to Australia and learnt about Asian food, I cooked in a Japanese restaurant, then I went to America. All of these different influences have come together and now I'm back in London cooking British food. So though I obviously can't directly replicate the way fish was cooked in the Japanese restaurant, I can take British fish and combine it with seaweed, and seaweed is one of the most underused of our

Details from Frans Snijders'
A Kitchen Still Life show a woman
shucking oysters in the fore-
ground and a maid preparing
food in the background, in
addition to a table loaded with
produce including beef, hare,
pigeon, goose and an array
of fruit and vegetables

ingredients and one of our biggest crops. I am a real believer in understatement and surprising people with my menu. I have someone who provides me with all of these amazing fresh ingredients – I call him my forager – and he finds me seaweed, herbs, mushrooms, wild cherries.

LG: I totally agree about understatement. So many places have overdone the importance of names and varieties, and while it is important to justify the price for ingredients, otherwise it is enough to know that good ingredients are appreciated. So for example when we have good aged Irish beef, the comments and compliments from the diners are good enough for me. I also like to use organic ingredients and to get English things – when they are in season. In England, we pride ourselves on our fruits or summer berries and I do think you should support the country in which you live.

JDW: Supermarkets have made people expect any ingredient at any time, so the principle of the seasonal produce is fine but, within reason, as one must keep in mind what people want. One of my favourite chefs, who ran the Merchant House in Ludlow, which was consistently voted one of the top restaurants, is hugely intelligent, English, cares about cooking, but in an article said that if he sees something at its peak, British seasonality is irrelevant. The seasonal thing is seen as such a new development, but in a sense it is only returning to the way things were before. In a painting like this by Snijders, it would have all been seasonal food though I imagine. Fresh things wouldn't have travelled then would they?

LG: I suppose they would have had to be dried or preserved in some way. I was looking and realised there are no potatoes shown, as they had only just started to appear in Europe in the 17th century.

JDW: That would have been one of the fascinating things about cooking at this time because you get these people returning from far away, bringing all of these weird and wonderful things back, like potatoes. We forget now that we can get anything and there is nothing really undiscovered.

LG: Some of these more common ingredients are also less frequently used, so something like the hare shown here is now something you rarely see.

JDW: Hare is wonderful, so different than the more popular rabbit, it is rich, gamey, dark and delicious.

LG: There does seem to be a great deal of game here, although I am surprised to see turkey but no chicken, unless I haven't spotted it. Combining the fruit with poultry always works well. For instance, this pigeon here with quince. Is there a quince in that fruit bowl do you think?

JDW: Have you ever cooked woodcock or snipe? Snipe have those long beaks and the classic way of doing it is to pluck and stuff the bird, then skewer it with its own beak. This picture looks very autumnal, with the game and the squash here at the back. For years I wouldn't touch it because I didn't know what to do. I think with some of these things you could create some very interesting vegetarian dishes. Not just as an additional option for vegetarians but as a dish in its own right.

LG: It is funny that some chefs are anti-vegetarian. We always have a vegetarian course with meat and fish and so often the vegetarian one sells out first. Even something like mushroom stock can give such a different flavour to a dish – it's meaty but does not dominate.

JDW: I can't see how it would be working in this kitchen. Imagine a dinner shift with that neck brace on?

LG: Yes and I can't believe this is a practical working kitchen with the meat and vegetables together like that. I suppose then they would have to use things as soon as they got them, with all the cooking done over an open fire.

JDW: It is so rare to cook over an open fire now. I have done it once in one restaurant I trained in and you really have to develop a feel for it and it's hard work because essentially you are standing in front of a huge fire. We would use it to cook everything on – venison, some of the meatier fish, and it imparted this wonderful taste.

LG: I think the woman's hands give you a hint of the level of drudgery. It makes you long for modern labour saving devices.

I would really struggle without a food mixer, when you have to do all that mixing by hand. When I trained one of the elements was learning to beat butter and sugar with a spoon so you had a feel of how it was before electrical equipment.

JDW: I think I would miss hot and cold running water. One of my least favourite jobs is cleaning up.

LG: I must admit there is such a large amount of meat in this picture it seems quite heavy and I am not sure I would turn to this painting for ideas. The type of food shown seems somewhat dated and I think, if I had to seek inspiration for a recipe from an artist, I would chose someone like Chagall. His combination of colours and textures would really appeal to me, rather than a direct illustration of certain ingredients. I love colour on a plate and I think when you write a recipe you start to imagine the feel of it in your mouth, and that leads you to add new textures.

JDW: I don't know which artists I might turn to for inspiration. I think I pick things up all the time from so many sources. When I'm at someone's house, or on holiday or reading books. I think as well a lot of inspiration comes from actually trying things out – you feel so many things through your taste buds.

LG: I think you can get the gist of recipe through tasting it. Something tastes good, but you know it needs a contrasting texture and taste to make it really work. You work hard to find inspiration – whatever the source – but ultimately the art of recipes is in the actual eating.

Boned quails are, perhaps, more convenient, but serving a whole bird gives this dish a greater impact

ROAST QUAIL, WILD RICE & MUSHROOM SAVOY PARCELS WITH PAPRIKA SAUCE

Serves 4 • Preparation time: 2 hours • Cooking time: 30 minutes • Pre-heat oven to 220 °C/ 425 °F/ gas-mark 7

4 quails

Savoy Parcels

100 g/ 4 oz Portabello mushrooms

50 g/ 2 oz/ ⅓ cup cooked wild rice

50 g/ 2 oz/ ⅓ cup cooked long grain rice

75 g/ 3 oz/ ½ cup caramelised onions (page 154)

1 tsp chopped fresh thyme

4 large blanched Savoy cabbage leaves, stems removed

To Serve

Paprika sauce (page 151)

First caramelise the onions (page 154).Place the mushrooms on a baking tray, season liberally and drizzle with olive oil. Cook in the oven for 10 minutes, then allow to cool and roughly chop. Mix together the mushrooms, rice, caramelised onions and the thyme, then season further to taste. Next, place the cabbage leaves flat on a work surface and arrange the rice mixture in the centre of each leaf. Fold into parcels, making sure they are properly sealed, wrap each one tightly in cling film and refrigerate for 1 hour.

Make the paprika sauce (page 151).

Season the birds inside and out. Heat some vegetable oil in a large frying pan. Brown the quails on all sides, which should take about 5 minutes, then place on a roasting tray in the oven for a further 7 minutes. Let them rest for 5 minutes.

Steam the Savoy cabbage parcels for 10 minutes, take care when removing the cling film, as the parcels get extremely hot. Place a quail and parcel on each plate and serve with hot paprika sauce.

Bought by the Historisches Museum, Basel in 1981, this two-part tapestry frieze, made in 1468 in northern Switzerland, remains the world auction record for a medieval tapestry at £550,000 ($1,227,875)

Butternut Squash Gnocchi with Pousse, Roast Tomatoes & Gorgonzola Sauce

Serves 4 • Preparation time: 1 hour • Cooking time: 50 minutes • Pre-heat oven to 200 ºC/ 400 ºC/ gas-mark 6

This sweet gnocchi contrasts with the salty flavour of the Gorgonzola and the sharpness of the tomatoes

Gnocchi

300 g/ 11 oz butternut squash, peeled and cut into chunks

100 g/ 4 oz/ ³/₄ cup caramelised onion (page 154)

¹/₄ tsp grated nutmeg

50 g/ 2 oz/ ¹/₂ cup Parmesan cheese, freshly grated

2 small eggs

75 g/ 3 oz/ ¹/₂ cup plain flour

5 sage leaves, finely chopped

Salad

300 g/ 11 oz roast cherry vine tomatoes (page 15)

50 g/ 2 oz washed pousse

Lemon oil (page 153)

Gorgonzola Sauce

(page 150)

Start by preparing the lemon oil (page 153) and the caramelised onions (page 154). Place the butternut squash on an oven tray with olive oil, salt and pepper, cover with foil and roast for 40 minutes until soft. Cool, then strain, discard the juice and place the squash in a food processor with the caramelised onions and process until smooth. Pour into a large mixing bowl and add the nutmeg, Parmesan, eggs, flour, sage leaves and a large pinch of salt and pepper. Stir until thoroughly mixed.

Bring a large saucepan of water to the boil and add 1 teaspoon of salt. Shape the gnocchi between 2 dessert spoons and carefully drop into the water, putting no more than eight gnocchi in the pan at one time, and reduce to a gentle simmer. Once the gnocchi are cooked they will rise to the top, continue to cook for 1 minute, then take out with a slotted spoon to drain any excess water, and place on a baking tray. Drizzle with a little olive oil and cook for 8 minutes. While these are cooking, roast the tomatoes (page 15) and prepare the Gorgonzola sauce (page 150).

Place the gnocchi on a plate and spoon over the Gorgonzola sauce. Dress the pousse with lemon oil, then arrange on top of the gnocchi with the roast tomatoes.

The distinct taste of skate is complemented by the equally
bold flavour of the chorizo

PAN-FRIED SKATE WITH CHORIZO, MUSSELS & KALE

Serves 4 • Preparation time: 1 hour • Cooking time: 15 minutes • Pre-heat oven to 220 °C/ 425 °F/ gas-mark 7

4 skate wing portions, 200 g/ 7 oz each

75 g/ 3 oz sliced cooking chorizo

50 ml/ 2 fl oz/ ¼ cup dry white wine

275 g/ 10 oz mussels, washed and debearded

50 g/ 2 oz unsalted butter

300 g/ 10 oz kale, blanched and drained

25 g/ 1 oz toasted pine nuts

25 g/ 1 oz currants

To Serve

Lemon oil (page 153)

Start by preparing the lemon oil (page 153). Heat a large ovenproof frying pan on a high flame and add some vegetable oil, then season the skate and brown for 1–2 minutes on each side. Drain the excess oil, add the chorizo to the skate and cook in the oven for 10–12 minutes. While the fish is cooking, heat a saucepan until extremely hot, pour in the wine and mussels and cover. The mussels should steam open in 3 minutes. Once cooked remove the pan from the heat, but keep covered. Melt the butter in a frying pan, add the kale and toss until hot, add the pine nuts, currants and season to taste.

Serve the kale on four plates, with a slotted spoon divide the mussels, then place the skate and chorizo on top. Finish with a drizzle of lemon oil over the fish.

Cafés of the Impressionists

Pablo Picasso's
Au Lapin Agile hung in
the eponymous café from
1905 to 1912, when it
was sold by the landlord
Frédé. This depiction of
the artist and his friends
was sold at Sotheby's
New York in 1990 for
$40,700,000
(£25,759,493)

The Parisian cafés were scenes of passionate debate between a disparate group of artists, later known as the Impressionists. Simon Shaw, the senior director of Sotheby's Impressionist and Modern Art department talks to Claire Joyes, author of *Les Carnets de Cuisine de Monet* and Mariel Oberthür, an art historian who specialises in the history of the cafés of Montmartre

Simon Shaw: The early days of Impressionism were closely linked with the 19th-century Parisian café scene, which was caught in the midst of Baron Haussmann's extraordinary facelift of the city.

Claire Joyes: It is difficult to follow the exact movements of any group in Paris at that time – artists arrived in the city in different waves, and frequented different studios and cafés. One could say that there was a core group, called the *Groupe des Batignolles*, formed around Edouard Manet at the Café Guerbois in 1869. Prior to this however, we know that from 1866 he frequented daily the Café de Bade, on the Boulevard des Italiens, as he wrote to Emile Zola in a letter that year; while Gustave Courbet held court at the Brasserie Andler, and the pupils of Charles Gleyre frequented the Café Fleurus, where the panels had been painted by Jean-Baptiste-Camille Corot. Claude Monet once said that frequenting the Batignolles had done him great harm. Perhaps this was due to the same society described by the historian Frimin Maillard in his book *Les Derniers Bohêmes: Henri Murger et Son Temps*: a mixture of 'reelers of rhymes, merchants of chimeras, knights of the quill and the brush.'

SS: Yet he recognised their significance, declaring in 1900 in *Le Temps*: 'Nothing could be more interesting than these *causeries* with their perpetual clash of opinions. They kept our wits sharpened, they encouraged us with stores of enthusiasm that for weeks and weeks kept us up, until the final shaping of the idea was accomplished. From them we emerged with a firmer will, with our thoughts clearer and more distinct'. Clearly Monet appreciated the ambivalent influence of the cafés on his life.

Mariel Oberthür: The cafés, in my opinion, represent one of the only places these young artists could meet. Besides the circus, which was becoming very popular at the time, there were few other distractions. The cafés took on the role of cultural houses, where the clientele was predominantly composed of musicians, writers, critics and politicians, all keen to discuss the burning issues of the day.

SS: I think this strengthens the view that Impressionism was created in the cafés. It was in the Café de la Nouvelle-Athènes and Café Guerbois – unpoliced and democratic spaces away from the École des Beaux-Arts and Salons – that the group discussed and established the foundations of their non-official art.

CJ: They disliked the over-polished art taught in the studios – as Monet disdainfully wrote in a letter to his family: 'it is hardly a pity that Couture has completely abandoned painting'.

SS: Effectively they were replacing the art history endorsed by the Académie, Jean-Dominique-Auguste Ingres, Thomas Couture and the other *maîtres*, with their own art history, which was extolled by Charles Baudelaire and Louis Edmond Duranty: the *vie moderne*. However, the Impressionists were a disparate group of artists. They each addressed the questions raised by these authors in very different ways. Manet, Edgar Degas, Henri de Toulouse-Lautrec, Pierre-Auguste Renoir and Monet each explored in their unique ways the aesthetic issues debated in the cafés.

CJ: I visited a fascinating exhibition in Paris this year that reflected this very issue. It displayed works by Paul Cézanne and Camille Pissarro, which the artists painted together in the surroundings of Pontoise. It is astonishing how dissimilar the landscapes are!

SS: The same can be said of Renoir and Monet's paintings of the Grenouillère, which they perceived with such different eyes.

CJ: Indeed, Monet chose to paint the cabins, the reflections in the water and those extraordinary ripples; while Renoir was more taken by the people. He was fascinated by facial expressions, body language and human countenance. It is a marvellous relationship. We could spend months discussing the ways in which artists reacted differently to the scenes of human drama that unfolded in these cafés.

MO: Current events had a huge presence in art. Here is an interesting story that shows their influence on Impressionism. At the 1867 Exposition Universelle a quarrel brewed regarding German and French beer, from which emerged the newspaper *Le Bon Bock*. It coupled convincing illustrations with articles extolling the beneficial effects of French beer or denigrating German beer. It is amusing that Manet alluded to this dispute in his 1873 painting *Le Bon Bock*.

SS: Impressionist paintings provide a great insight into daily life, many of which find their inspiration in the Paris entertainment world, from Manet's *Un Bar aux Folies-Bergère* (1882) and Renoir's *Au Moulin de la Galette* (1876) to Picasso's *Au Lapin Agile* (1905). These all reveal different forms of nightlife and it is interesting to compare the different worlds evoked in these paintings.

MO: The Moulin de la Galette was an old windmill that was converted into a ballroom around 1830. It was not very successful until after the Franco-Prussian war of 1870 and the fall of the *Commune*, which was around the time Renoir painted it.

SS: With the gas lights, one recognises Haussmann's influence immediately. Just as it is apparent in paintings such as Jean Béraud's 1878 outdoor depiction *Le Boulevard Montmartre Animé Devant le Théâtre des Variétés*, in which the broad remodelled pavement is crowded with the elegant theatre crowd, café regulars and *flâneurs*.

MO: That picture depicts Haussmann's radical transformation of Paris. Montmartre mostly retained a rather rural identity, though it did experience some important changes. In 1860 the 18th-century city wall was pulled down, linking upper Montmartre with lower Montmartre – today's 18th and 9th *arrondissements* – and the whole area was integrated into the city. In those days the *butte*, or hill, of Montmartre was a real rabbit warren, a labyrinth of century-old quarries that weakened the hill. Haussmann's urban modernisations served to consolidate it but did not affect it otherwise. The *guinguettes* – open-air cafés or dancehalls – situated outside the city walls had attracted Parisian crowds for many years. However, the Impressionists only began frequenting these later on.

The extension of the omnibus lines to the Batignolles and Pigalle opened up the Paris map. The Cabaret du Chat Noir drew crowds day and night – not only artists, but bourgeois and aristocrats. Contrary to popular belief, it was a respectable place where a man could bring his wife; certainly not somewhere to pick up women. If one required a *cabinet particulier* – as intimated in the 1899 painting by Toulouse-Lautrec – the Rat Mort or L'Abbaye de Thélème would accommodate those desires. The Lapin Agile, mentioned earlier, attracted different sorts. This café sat on the edge of an area called the *maquis*, a drift of lopsided shacks, stacked one on top of the other.

SS: The Impressario Aristide Bruant bought the Lapin Agile in 1903. When the infamous Frédé took on the lease in 1904, Picasso and his friends Maurice de Vlaminck, Kees Van Dongen, Max Jacob, Marie Laurencin, Guillaume Apollinaire and Amedeo Modigliani – all *habitués* of Frédé's previous café *Le Zut* – followed him there. Like other painters, Picasso donated a picture to the café for a bit of advertising. This painting was *Au Lapin Agile*, painted in 1905, and sold in New York in 1990 for $40,700,000. As a matter of fact, Frédé can be seen at the back of the painting, strumming on his guitar. Picasso is seated in the foreground in a harlequin outfit, and in between them sits Germaine Pichot, the *femme fatale* more or less responsible for the suicide of Picasso's friend Carlos Casagemas, who had moved with him to Paris in 1900. It is a haunting picture, very introspective – it hung on the walls of the Lapin Agile until 1912, when Frédé sold it to a German buyer for what he believed to be an excellent price. Picasso, on the other hand, knew very well that Frédé had been ripped off!

CJ: Incredible! This painting is quite different to Degas' depictions of café life; he was more attracted by the café-concert. As a bourgeois, cafés were not his natural milieu; they were almost an exotic voyage that provided company and inspiration.

SS: He was attracted by performers, singers and dancers of the café-concert, often depicting the celebrities of the day. There is much more movement in his pictures than in Manet's – Degas' figures are dancing and singing, while Manet's are often static.

MO: There was no electricity in the cafés at that time. Gas or oil lamps were placed around the stage, which explains how in many of Degas' paintings, the light comes from below.

CJ: Gas lighting is extraordinarily white – it gives such a ghostly appearance to the performers and Degas obviously appreciated these theatrical effects. Did he hang his paintings in these places?

MO: Certainly. Cafés were one of the only places artists could exhibit, since they rarely did in the official Salons. Many shows were held at the Brasserie des Martyrs, Vincent Van Gogh organised an exhibition in the Café du Tambourin and Degas is known to have hung a pastel at the Chat Noir.

SS: Among the restaurateurs, the Impressionists found further help in Eugène Murer, who asked Renoir and Pissarro to decorate his restaurant. He frequently offered dinner to the artists and their friends in exchange for works of art. Equally, during the war, in Montparnasse, the proprietors of the Rotonde and the Coupole often accepted works by Chaïm Soutine or Modigliani in payment.

CJ: It was more of a habit in Montparnasse, where artists, such as Man Ray, swapped their works. Ultimately, though sales in paintings were often dismal, artists would always find ways of making ends meet. I recall an anecdote – often recounted during family dinners – that Monet used to tell his children. Apparently he and his friends frequented a restaurant run by a certain Mr Fromage, who served the remains of cheeses bought from cheese merchants. His restaurant had such a lowly clientele that the cutlery was chained to the tables. There must have been many pathetic places such as this.

MO: Yet from the menus that survive today, we know that some cafés served excellent food. Whether they could afford it, is another question. A menu from the Rat Mort in 1890–92, offered mixed hors d'œuvres, tapioca, hollandaise sauce, leg of venison, roasted fatted chicken, salad, cheese, dessert, champagne and a Bordeaux Château Larose 1888. This is all extremely rich food – still, for the artists, as Claire points out, it remained a day-by-day struggle.

CJ: That said, as they got older, they had more means of pleasing themselves. Monet certainly loved his rich foods, such as *terrines* or *pâtés en croûte*. He was very curious when it came to preparing food; and I can tell you that he loved English cooking! However, in the 1870s, the war had wiped out France's resources and aside from Paul Durand-Ruel, who was a true patron of the arts, collectors were scant. Monet appealed to him countless times for loans.

SS: Manet also helped him out enormously when he bought ten pictures of his for 1,000 francs; and Frédéric Bazille and Gustave Caillebotte were both of great support to their friends.

CJ: The Salon jury refused Renoir's famous painting *Femmes au Jardin* in 1867, and Bazille bought it in instalments for 2,500 francs – an astronomical sum in those days! Even so, one must be careful not to over-dramatise. I really dislike the notion of pauperism that is so often alluded to in studies of their lives. For the most part, the artists came from respectable families, who gave them little monetary support. Yet some legends ought to be stifled; these artists remained dignified in their difficulties.

SS: There was a strong solidarity between the members of the *Groupe des Batignolles*, perhaps a result of weathering the early years of Impressionism together. It was after all a common struggle – a struggle that sustained the Impressionist movement.

CJ: Indeed, after breaking with the Académie they had a strong need for intellectual recognition, which was bestowed grudgingly over the years. This was undoubtedly a cohesive factor for their group.

SS: And as a group they found solutions to their problems, discussed the possibilities of exhibiting together and argued over their conflicting theories of art. Together they really did create the painting of modern life.

Pierre-Auguste Renoir's *Au Moulin de la Galette* (detail), 1876, depicts one of the *guinguettes* where the Parisian *beau monde* would congregate. It is one of the most recognisable images of Impressionism and was sold in New York in May 1990 for $78,100,000 (£46,213,017)

The apple fritters combine well with the brulées and add a necessary crunchiness to the custard dessert

Calvados Brulées with Apple Fritters

Serves 5 • Preparation time: 30 minutes • Cooking time: 15 minutes
• Setting time: 3 hours • Pre-heat oven to 180 °C/ 350 °F/ gas-mark 4 • Heat oil to 190 °C/ 375 °F

Brulées

1 vanilla pod

500 ml/ 17 fl oz/ 2 cups double cream

6 egg yolks

100 g/ 3½ oz/ ½ cup caster sugar

3½ dessert spoons Calvados

Extra caster sugar for caramel

Apple Fritters

Beer batter (page 154)

1 Cox's apple, peeled, cored and sliced into 10 pieces

300 ml/ ½ pint vegetable oil for deep frying

To Serve

Icing sugar

To start, split the vanilla pod lengthwise, scrape out the seeds and add pod and seeds to the double cream, bring to simmering point and then take off the heat. Whisk the egg yolks and sugar until light and fluffy, and carefully mix in the hot cream. Pour into a clean pan and stir continuously over a low heat until the custard starts to thicken, but do not let it boil. Remove from the heat and stir in the Calvados. Strain the cream through a sieve into five ramekins. Place them in a deep oven tray, half-filled with freshly boiled water. Cover with foil and cook for 10 minutes. When cooked remove from the water and cool for 1 hour before placing them in the fridge to set for 2 hours.

Prepare the batter for the fritters (page 154).

Sprinkle the extra sugar over the brulées and caramelise the surface with a blow-torch – alternatively, cook them under a hot grill and then chill in the freezer for 10 minutes.

Heat the oil in a deep fryer, dip the apples into the batter. Cook the fritters in the hot oil for 2–3 minutes or until golden and crisp. Dust with icing sugar and serve with the brulées.

The first owner of La Valse Hésitation from 1955 was Mrs Van Den Broeck the proprietress of 'Vincent', a favourite restaurant of the artist René Magritte' on the Rue des Dominicains in Brussels. This gouache on paper, with the familiar symbol of the apple, was sold for $912,000 (£498,235), in New York in May, 2006

Sticky Date Pudding with Toffee Sauce & Marmalade Ice Cream

Serves 6 • Preparation time: 30 minutes • Cooking time: 25 minutes • Pre-heat oven to 190 ºC/ 375 ºF/ gas-mark 5

This is a deceptively light pudding considering the richness of the dates, toffee and marmalade

Sticky Date Pudding

Melted butter for lining ramekins

75 g/ 3 oz/ ³/₄ cup unsalted butter

Zest of 1 orange

75 g/ 3 oz/ ³/₄ cup caster sugar

2 beaten eggs

150 g/ 5 oz/ 1 cup sifted self-raising flour

150 ml/ ¹/₄ pint/ ²/₃ cup water

100 g/ 4 oz/ ³/₄ cup dates, pitted and chopped

1 level tsp bicarbonate of soda

Toffee Sauce

(page 152)

Marmalade Ice Cream

(page 157)

First make the marmalade ice cream (page 156) and the toffee sauce (page 152). Lightly butter six ramekins. In a large bowl, cream together the butter and orange zest with an electric whisk until it is light and fluffy. Add the sugar and mix for another 5–10 minutes. Slowly add the eggs and fold in the flour. Set aside.

Bring the water to the boil in a saucepan and add the dates, remove the pan from the heat and leave for 3 minutes while the dates soften, then add the bicarbonate of soda. Stir the date and the creamed mixture together. Divide between the buttered ramekins, filling them three quarters of the way up. Place on a baking tray and cook in the oven for 20–25 minutes until risen and golden.

Serve the puddings with a generous scoop of marmalade ice cream and pour over the hot toffee sauce.

Chocolate & Cherry Fondant with Crème Fraîche

Serves 4–5 • Preparation time: 15 minutes • Cooking time: 8 minutes
• Pre-heat oven to 220 ºC/ 425 ºF/ gas-mark 7

This is a simple yet impressive dessert and the addition of cherries really complements the rich chocolate

Melted butter for lining ramekins

3 egg yolks

2 egg whites

75 g/ 3 oz/ ⅓ cup caster sugar

75 g/ 3 oz unsalted butter

75 g/ 3 oz/ ½ cup chopped dark chocolate

1 heaped dessert spoon cocoa powder

50 g/ 2 oz/ ½ cup sifted plain flour

50 g/ 2 oz/ ½ cup halved cherries in Kirsch

To Serve

Crème fraîche

Icing sugar

Lightly butter four ramekins. Whisk the egg yolks, egg whites and sugar together until they are light and fluffy; this takes around 8 minutes. In a saucepan, gently melt the butter, chocolate and cocoa stirring constantly, without allowing it to boil. Pour the mixture into a bowl, and with a large metal spoon, gently fold in the egg mixture, the flour and the cherries. Divide between the ramekins and cook in the oven for 7–8 minutes.

Turn the pudding out onto plates and serve with crème fraîche and a dusting of icing sugar.

The inscription 'My Wallis from her David 19.VI.36' on the clasp of this ruby and diamond necklace by Van Cleef & Arpels records that it was a gift from Edward VIII to Wallis Simpson on her 40th birthday. It sold for SF3,905,000 (£1,606,996; $2,603,333) in the Jewels of the Duchess of Windsor sale in Geneva in 1987

WINE THROUGH THE SEASONS

AUTUMN

by Serena Sutcliffe MW

The season of mellow fruitfulness means the harvest in the wine world, whether it is in Europe or the southern hemisphere. The culmination of a year's work in the vineyard can be dramatic, praying to Bacchic gods that the weather does not break before all the grapes are gathered, sometimes racing against time, or else risking all and waiting for optimum ripeness. Large groups of pickers move over famous vineyards, family and friends pitch in at small properties, while machines do the work in many huge estates producing wine at reasonable prices. The grapes arrive in the cellars for pressing and fermentation and the must becomes wine. This may sound biblical, but there is science in there too, with analyses, temperature control and decisions to be taken at every turn. It is now that the winemaker will know how much he has made – small berries with thick skins produce less, but more intense, wine than large berries.

For those who visit wineries at this time, the scent of juice fermenting is intoxicating. As the new wine is run off from the fermenting vats, the air is heady with fruit and alcohol. The knowledgeable murmur about the colour of the red wines, which can vary from clear ruby to dark black, according to the region and grape variety, while the real professionals bandy words such as extraction, maceration and concentration. You will see everything from large stainless steel vats to beautiful (and expensive) new oak barrels – and you will also observe lots of water sloshing about, as cleanliness is next to godliness when making wine.

The very last grapes to be picked are those that will make the world's great sweet wines in Sauternes, Germany or Hungary. The morning mists come down, creating the right conditions for these vinous miracles to be born, with painstaking picking of individual bunches, or even selected overripe berries. The golden juice will often ferment for months, the yeasts struggling with the rich, liqueur-like sugar.

Autumn means golden colours in the vineyard and a sense of accomplishment as the year's vineyard work becomes liquid. At the end of the harvest, it also means festivals and bucolic meals to celebrate the result of all the hard labour. The most picturesque of these feasts tend to be in wine areas where the picking is still entirely by hand, such as in Champagne, when the traditional *cochelet* lends itself to unbridled enjoyment, as well it should.

Ripe Merlot grapes on the brink of harvest at Château Pétrus

MENUS

by Laura Greenfield

Seared Venison, Roast Tomatoes,
Balsamic Syrup & Parmesan Straws

Roast Fillet of Salmon,
Globe Artichoke, Feta & Lemon Risotto
with Beetroot Relish

Calvados Brulées with Apple Fritters

Borscht with Sour Cream & Dill

Roast Quail,
Wild Rice & Mushroom Savoy Parcels
with Paprika Sauce

Chocolate & Cherry Fondant
with Crème Fraîche

AUTUMN WINES

by Serena Sutcliffe MW

STARTERS

These are big, bold starters and they can take some feisty wines. Try a Manzanilla with the borscht, a sleek Sauvignon Blanc from Styria in Austria with the smoked haddock soufflé and really let rip with the venison – a cool glass of Morellino di Scansano from Tuscany will set the taste buds tingling.

MAINS

The roast fillet of salmon needs a rich white Burgundy to show it off – and never mind those who say that artichokes are a killer with wine – I am still alive! The same Meursault, Puligny or Chassagne-Montrachet would go neatly with the butternut gnocchi too. Pan-fried skate is livened up with spicy chorizo and the sweetness of the currants – a white Rioja would cope well with this mosaic of tastes. Roast quail and its accessories could take a vibrant Faugères from France's Languedoc, or a bright Austrian red Blaufränkisch.

DESSERTS

Cherries and chocolate simply cry out for chilled Maury, one of Roussillon's prized Vins Doux Naturels, and the perfect partner here. What could be better with apple fritters than a Calvados Vieille Réserve, while a glass of orangey Sauternes would offset the marmalade ice cream and sticky date pudding.

WINTER

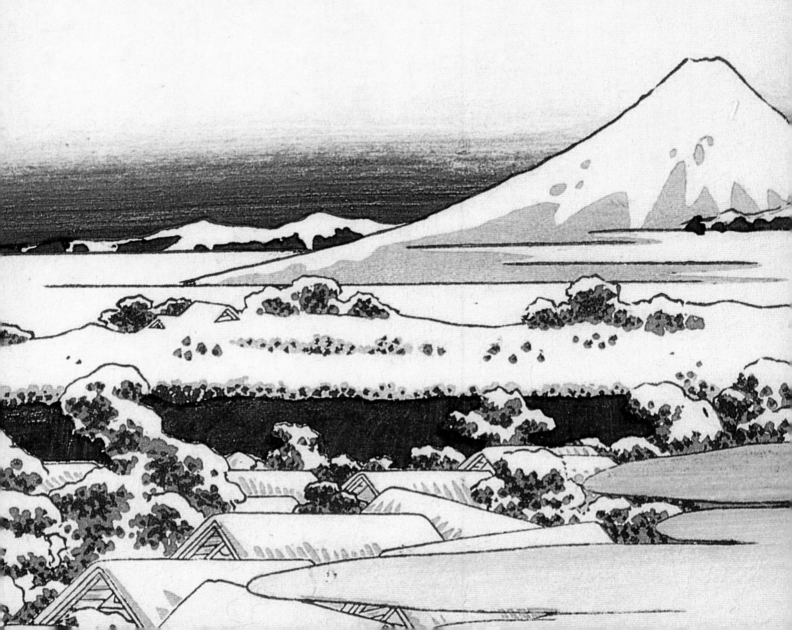

View from Koishikawa on a Snowy Morning, one of the designs from Katsushika Hokusai's famous series Thirty-six Views of Mount Fuji, sold as part of a complete set for €1,490,750 (£954,825; $1,478,919) in Paris in 2002. A master of landscape *ukiyo-e* (pictures of a floating world), Hokusai captures his most famous subject, Mount Fuji, on a wintry day

Always cook scallops quickly to obtain a golden crust and succulent core and, when possible, use diver-caught scallops for their superior quality

Seared Scallops with Puy Lentils, Rocket & Chive Oil

Serves 4 • Preparation time: 25 minutes • Cooking time: 30 minutes

12 large scallops, corals removed

Puy Lentils

2 dessert spoons finely chopped carrot

2 dessert spoons finely chopped leek

2 dessert spoons finely chopped shallot

½ clove finely chopped garlic

3 sprigs thyme

50 g/ 2 oz/ ⅓ cups Puy lentils

Splash of white wine

400 ml/ 14 fl oz/ 1¾ cups chicken stock (page 154)

1 dessert spoon sherry vinegar

To Serve

25 g/ 1 oz rocket

Chive oil (page 153)

First make the chicken stock (page 154). Heat a little olive oil in a medium sized pan, add the chopped vegetables and stir occasionally until soft. Add the garlic and thyme and cook further for a minute. Turn up the heat and add the lentils and white wine, reduce to almost nothing, then add the chicken stock, turn down the heat and cook until the lentils are *al dente*. Take off the heat, discard the thyme, add the sherry vinegar and season to taste.

Prepare the chive oil (page 153).

Add some vegetable oil to a hot pan, season the scallops and cook for a minute on each side until they are golden brown.

Spoon the lentils onto the centre of each serving plate. Place the rocket neatly on top, arrange the scallops around and drizzle with the chive oil.

Juste-Aurèle Meissonnier created this shell-form and barnacle-encrusted tureen for the second Duke of Kingston in 1735. It achieved the second highest price ever for a piece of silver at auction selling for £3,490,725 ($5,722,500) in New York in 1998

This starter could become a light lunch by increasing the amount of mushrooms and serving with a salad

SOUFFLÉ POTATO PANCAKE WITH WILD MUSHROOMS & SHALLOT SAUCE

Serves 6 • Preparation time: 1½ hours • Cooking time: 30 minutes • Pre-heat oven to 200 ºC/ 400 ºF/ gas-mark 6

Pancakes

45 ml/ 1½ fl oz/ ⅙ cup milk

45 ml/ 1½ fl oz/ ⅙ cup double cream

150 g/ 5 oz mashed potatoes

45 g/ 1½ oz/ ¼ cup self-raising flour

¼ tsp baking powder

2 eggs, separated

3 pinches of salt, pepper and freshly grated nutmeg

Mushrooms

350 g/ 12 oz mixed wild mushrooms

1 clove garlic, finely chopped

100 g/ 4 oz button onions

1 dessert spoon chopped chives

1 dessert spoon chopped flat leaf parsley

1 dessert spoon chopped chervil

Shallot Sauce

(page 152)

First make the shallot sauce (page 152). Next put the button onions on an oven tray, season and drizzle with olive oil. Cover with foil and cook for 15–20 minutes or until soft.

For the pancakes, warm the milk and cream then pour into a large mixing bowl with the mashed potatoes. Add the flour, baking powder, egg yolks and nutmeg, then season and whisk until smooth. Beat the egg whites until stiff and gently fold into the potato mix with a large metal spoon. Coat a large frying pan with vegetable oil and heat. Being careful not to overfill the pan, spoon enough mixture to make an 8–10 cm. (3–4 in.) diameter pancake, cook on a reduced heat until the underside is golden brown. Turn over with a palette knife and cook for another minute before placing it on a large oven tray lined with baking parchment. Repeat this process until you have made six pancakes, then place them in the oven for 7 minutes.

Brush off any dirt from the mushrooms with a piece of kitchen paper or a pastry brush. Cut to a uniform size so they cook evenly. Re-heat the frying pan with some olive oil and sauté the wild mushrooms on a high heat until golden brown. Add the garlic, button onions and a little butter. Remove from the heat, stir in the chopped herbs and season to taste.

Re-heat the shallot sauce. Remove the soufflé pancakes from the oven and serve with the wild mushrooms, finish with the shallot sauce on the side.

The sweetness of cooked red onions is ideally suited for marmalade and tastes delicious with duck liver

Potted Duck Livers, Melba Toast & Red Onion Marmalade

Serves 4 • Preparation time: 45 minutes • Cooking time: 30 minutes • Pre-heat oven to 180 ºC/ 350 ºF/ gas-mark 4

Duck Livers

100 ml/ 4 fl oz/ ½ cup clarified butter (page 155)

1 shallot, finely chopped

1 pinch of cayenne pepper

2 pinches of ground mace

1 heaped dessert spoon chopped chervil

1 heaped dessert spoon chopped chives

1 heaped dessert spoon chopped tarragon

350 g/ 12 oz trimmed duck livers

To Serve

4 slices white bread for Melba toast

Red onion marmalade (page 157)

First make the clarified butter (page 155) and red onion marmalade (page 157). Gently heat the clarified butter and add the shallot, cayenne pepper, mace and a large pinch of salt. Cook until the shallot has softened; do not let the butter boil. Add the chopped herbs and set aside. Season the livers and heat some vegetable oil in a frying pan. Once hot, cook the livers until they are golden brown on both sides but slightly pink in the middle, this should take 2–3 minutes. Remove with a slotted spoon, then add to the butter mix and stir gently. Divide between four ramekins, leave to cool and refrigerate.

Toast the bread and remove the crusts. Split each slice horizontally with a serrated knife and scrape off the soft dough. Quarter into triangles and cook in the oven until golden brown and slightly curled at the edges.

Serve at room temperature with red onion marmalade and Melba toast.

In L'Oiseau Boum-Boum Fait sa Prière à la Tête Pelure d'Oignon, the boum-boum bird, Joan Miró's fantastical creation, has just alighted on a brittle onion stalk. Dated 1952, this abstract dreamscape sold in November 2002 at the Impressionist and Modern Art auction in New York for $2,154,500 (£1,377,029)

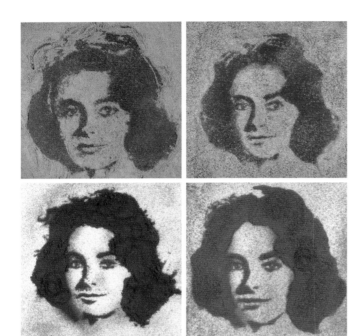

Vik Muniz spins Warhol's famous images, by re-working them using materials such as cayenne, black pepper, curry powder and chilli pepper, seen in *Liz* from 1999. It was sold for $60,000 (£35,857) at the Sotheby's Contemporary art sale in New York in 2003

FO: You showed a bronze tree with real apples in the 2003 Turner Prize, can you elaborate on this fusion of traditional and perishable matter and how you see your future use of materials?

AG: I was attracted to the art-historical significance and gravitas of bronze as a permanent material and to playing with the choice of objects that I cast. For instance, the 9-foot rosehips I'm making now may not be initially picturesque or may have gone unnoticed in their original context, but they are transformed by this labour-intensive and decadent process. It is a logical extension of my work, casting trees in bronze enables me to provide a stable armature from which to hang real apples which are obviously unstable and will rot, drip and react with the bronze.

I have also been working on a 'Terroir' project, in Sonoma, California, making six distinct Zinfandel wines with the intention of creating an embodiment of the landscape at a particular moment in time.

FO: You've used a lot of food in your art over the years, are you much of a cook?

AG: I love cooking, as I can be more spontaneous and gauge the success of the endeavour instantly, whereas a lot of my projects are protracted by the time spent planning and anticipating. For me, the elements that make a successful meal apply to my practice – it's a combination of me, the material, the place and the experience. If you alter one element, or change the context, the piece shifts slightly. Materially, *Brown and White* and *Stroke* are the same piece of work – they are both chocolate rooms, but as the site differs, so does the work, or how I respond to it, or how the audience reacts. With the first piece in Vienna, 1993, everyone engaged with it sensually by licking and rubbing their noses in the chocolate walls, but with the second piece in London, 1994, the interaction was more furtive.

FO: You are inverting the idea that sculpture exists in one shape, by showing it to be temporal. How do you document that?

AG: I photograph the work as proof of my activity because after years of making work I felt I had nothing to show, apart from a few slides. I'm suspicious of the seductive nature of photography, you always end up having one iconic shot of a piece of work. You can see my work at the beginning, middle or end; you are part of a process and that isn't necessarily evident in the moment frozen by a photograph. We experience the world so much now through a screen or through magazines when the smelly, messy reality of physically engaging with the work is a totally different experience. That relates to my approach to materials – it's about the joy of it and somehow trying to let the material be itself without transforming it.

Alexander Rotter: Your early work contained sculptural elements and mixed media drawings – how did you begin to work with food?

Vik Muniz: I am still attached to drawing and sculpture, but when I began to work with photography I became aware of the element of time involved in the process. I like working with mutable forms that justify the photographic act in my work, which I began to use in my *Pictures of Dust* and *Pictures of Thread* in the 1990s – if you don't capture it at that precise moment, it changes and will never be the same again. Using perishable materials – although I don't always like to think of it as food – adds an interesting character to the photograph. I use paints, powders, gooey stuff and liquids in the studio, but in the kitchen, I have an infinity of materials. The relationship between the use of vision and food is complex – we engage in all sorts of stimuli to identify and define food – and that is appealing for an artist, this has been seen since 16th or 17th-century still lifes. This relationship between material, form and image is a primary concern.

AR: How does your work address the references we attach to food?

VM: The Bosco chocolate syrup, which I used in the *Pictures of Chocolate* series in 1997–99, has a painterly quality, but chocolate also inspires a multitude of pyschological meanings. When you apply that to different imagery, the material alters the image itself and we are susceptible to that change. Everyone also has their own feelings or interpretations of chocolate which they bring to the work.

AR: In the *Sugar Children* from 1999, you depict the faces of children from St Kitts using the material that will determine their lives through the plantations. Does the food element give way to a political interpretation?

VM: I reached my maturity as a visual artist in the mid 1980s to mid 1990s when art was overtly political. I don't really think politics is the business of art. When I created these children with a material that they depend upon, I wasn't thinking of politics, I was trying to express what I was seeing, although that in itself becomes a frame of reference, which can create unexpected political undertones. One thing connects to another and meanings ricochet around in my work, the more complex things get, the more attractive it becomes for me.

AR: Do you think that people react differently to art made with anomalous materials?

VM: I find that people can be narrow-minded about how art is made, when if you think about it, all materials originate from somewhere: banana oil or rabbit skin glue or the powder from mummies which has been used to make tones of brown. I'm working on *Pictures of Pigments* now, looking at the pure forms of colour: purple comes from the shell of rare snails and some dyes are made from plants or blood. Who knows what was used to paint the Madonna and Child throughout the ages? By depicting images using an edible substance, which is meaningful to everyone, the focus shifts to the exact moment when the concoction of colours, texture and matter becomes a likeness of something and then the image reverts to being a material. That moment of realisation is sublime.

AR: Can this mass appeal be illustrated by your investigation into Warhol's serial images, using peanut butter and jelly or spices, as he appropriated everyday images?

VM: Exactly. Warhol made you see everything for what it was by simplifying it to a pure image. My idea was to bring materiality back to the flatness. I'm interested in the icons or archetypes that everybody knows and understands – they are powerful vehicles for an artist to work with. I saw the *Mona Lisa* at the Louvre, along with at least 3,000 people all taking pictures of it and then Warhol's double *Mona Lisa* from 1963 turns it into a ridiculous pattern. I made *Mona Lisa* for the show 'After Warhol' at the Renos Xippas Gallery in 1999, working with that vulgarisation of this icon by using the most generic thing: peanut butter and jelly [sandwiches], which to me, is not something that you enjoy eating and is more about nutrition than gastronomy.

AR: Do your likes or dislikes of food affect your use of them?

VM: I don't have a preference for a particular material, in the same way that a painter would not have a preference for one colour. With the *Pictures of Diamonds* and *Caviar Monsters* which I made in 2003, there is the added pleasure of these rare and expensive products. Usually my drawings end up in the garbage once they have been photographed, but with the Caviar series, only Iranian Beluga produced really good pictures, so the cost was ridiculous – we had to eat them afterwards and prepared blinis right next to the picture, ready to go. My choice of material has more to do with how it relates to a specific image, rather than creating something with a clear connection – I like to leave it a bit ambiguous.

AR: How has food as a material impacted on your art practice?

VM: Using food is only part of what I do. But, it projects me into the sphere of people who have a fascination with it. When I photographed *Earth Works* in 2002, I worked with people who have mines from Brazil to Poland, and I collaborated with Intel to produce the smallest drawings ever made on grains of sand in 2001, all of which project me in completely different directions. That's what's fascinating about being an artist, you can experiment with absurd ideas and you don't have to be anything specific. Great art somehow embraces and shows the whole of human knowledge. You can see the entire universe in Monet's flowers – they make you see everything through the particular.

Monkfish, like skate, is a robust fish. It should not flake when in the broth and will blend well with the rustic character of the chickpeas

ROAST MONKFISH, CHICKPEA & TOMATO BROTH
WITH BLACK CABBAGE & PIQUILLO PEPPER AIOLI

Serves 4 • Preparation time: 40 minutes • Cooking time: 25 minutes • Pre-heat oven to 200 ºC/ 400 ºF/ gas-mark 6

4 monkfish tails, 175 g/ 6 oz each

Chickpea and Tomato Broth

1 red onion peeled and roughly diced

1 dessert spoon tomato purée

Sprigs of rosemary

2 garlic cloves, finely chopped

1 small red chilli, finely chopped (optional)

1 tsp paprika

125 g/ 4 oz quartered cherry vine tomatoes

225 g/ 8 oz/ 1 cup cooked chickpeas,
with cooking liquor kept aside

Juice and zest of ½ lemon

Black Cabbage

175 g/ 6 oz blanched black cabbage,
stalks removed

To Serve

Handful of roughly chopped flat leaf parsley

Piquillo pepper aioli (page 150)

Croutes (page 155)

First make the croutes (page 155) and the Piquillo pepper aioli (page 150). For the broth, heat some olive oil in a saucepan and add the red onion, stirring occasionally until soft but not browned. Add the tomato purée, rosemary, garlic, chilli and paprika and stir over a low heat for 1 minute. Add the cherry tomatoes, chickpeas and pour in the chickpea cooking liquid to cover the ingredients. Cover and simmer for 10 minutes over a medium heat. When cooked, add the lemon juice and zest and season to taste. Keep warm.

Heat a little vegetable oil, season the monkfish on both sides and cook until golden. Transfer to a tray and place in the oven for 8 minutes. During this time, re-heat the cabbage in a pan of hot water.

Ladle the chickpea broth into deep bowls, place the cabbage in the middle and the monkfish on top. Sprinkle with chopped parsley and serve with Piquillo pepper aioli and croutes.

Brazilian Fish, a creation of painted sheet metal, wire, metal, broken pottery and glass by Alexander Calder made in circa 1947, set a world record for the artist at auction when it sold for $3,907,500 (£2,383,575) in the New York Contemporary Art sale in November 1999

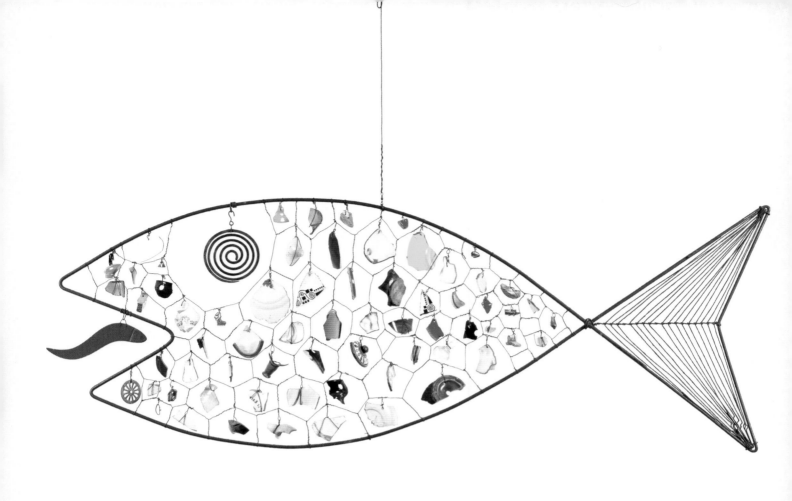

The unique creaminess of the Colston Basset Stilton adds a marvellous texture to these beignets

Colston Basset Stilton Beignets with a Celery, Baby Spinach & Pecan Salad with Moscatel Dressing

Serves 4 • Preparation time: 40 minutes • Cooking time: 10 minutes • Heat oil to 180 °C/ 360 °F

Stilton Beignets

200 ml/ 7 fl oz/ ¾ cup water

75 g/ 3 oz butter

¼ tsp salt

¼ tsp ground black pepper

100 g/ 3½ oz/ ¾ cup sifted plain flour

1½ heaped tsp Dijon mustard

225 g/ 8 oz crumbled Colston Basset Stilton

3 eggs

1 litre/ 1¾ pints/ 4 cups vegetable oil for deep frying

Salad

1 celery stick, finely sliced

75 g/ 3 oz washed baby spinach

1 pear, peeled, cored and finely sliced

Handful of roughly chopped pecans

Handful of golden raisins

Moscatel dressing (page 153)

Heat the water, butter, salt and pepper in a saucepan. Once boiled remove from the heat, add the flour and beat thoroughly until the mix comes away from the sides of the pan. Cool for 5 minutes. Add the mustard and Stilton, stir well and then beat the eggs in one by one.

Pre-heat the oil in a deep fat fryer. Carefully drop dessert spoons of the mixture into the oil, taking care not to overcrowd the fryer. Cook for 2–3 minutes until golden brown and then lift out with a slotted spoon onto kitchen paper. This should make 16 beignets.

Prepare the Moscatel dressing (page 153).

Mix the celery, spinach, pear, pecans and raisins together in a salad bowl, pour over the dressing and serve with the beignets.

The inspiration for this dish derives from Middle Eastern cuisine, in which the warm and pungent flavour of cumin is widely used in marinades and meat casseroles

Cumin & Coriander Marinated Chicken
With Roast Sweet Potatoes, Red Onion & Tomato Salad

Serves 4 • Preparation time: 1 hour • Cooking time: 40 minutes • Pre-heat oven to 200 °C/ 400 °F/ gas-mark 6

Marinated Chicken

2 dessert spoons olive oil

1 tsp ground cumin seeds

1 tsp ground coriander seeds

$^1/_2$ tsp paprika

2 dessert spoons chopped coriander stalks

1 garlic clove, finely chopped

1 crushed dried chilli

Zest of 2 lemons

4 corn-fed chicken breasts

Roast Sweet Potatoes

750 g/ 1$^1/_2$ lb sweet potatoes, cleaned and cut into wedges

2 crushed dried chillies

2 garlic cloves, finely chopped

Salad

300 g/ 11 oz quartered cherry tomatoes

1 small red onion, peeled and finely sliced

2 dessert spoons roughly chopped flat leaf parsley

2 dessert spoons roughly chopped coriander

Lemon oil (page 153)

Mix the olive oil, ground cumin and coriander, paprika, coriander stalks, garlic, chilli and lemon zest in a bowl, add the chicken and coat it evenly with the herbs and spices. Leave to marinate for at least 1 hour.

Put the sweet potatoes onto an oven tray, drizzle with a little olive oil and sprinkle on the chillies and garlic. Season and roast for 30–40 minutes until soft and lightly browned.

Prepare the lemon oil (page 153), then mix the tomatoes, red onion, parsley and coriander and add the lemon oil, then season to taste.

Heat a frying pan, season the chicken and cook skin side down until golden, then turn over and repeat the process. Cook gently to ensure the marinade does not burn. Transfer to an oven tray and cook for a further 20–25 minutes.

Serve the chicken breasts on four plates alongside the sweet potatoes and salad.

This illustrated leaf depicting Hamza and his companions taking refreshments in their battle armour is from a royal manuscript of the Siyar-I Nabi recounting the life of the Prophet Muhammad. It was created for the Ottoman ruler, Sultan Murad III, in Constantinople in 1594–95 and was sold in London for £55,200 ($96,356) in the Arts of the Islamic World sale in April 2006

The succulent rib-eye is a good choice over the fillet cut because of its marbling and flavour

PEPPERCORN RIB-EYE STEAK, RED ONION TART TATINS & SOUR CREAM

Serves 4 • Preparation time: 40 minutes • Cooking time: 50 minutes • Pre-heat oven to 180 °C/ 350 °F/ gas-mark 4

Peppercorn Steak

1 heaped dessert spoon roughly crushed black peppercorns

4 rib-eye steaks, 175 g/ 6 oz each

25 g/ 1 oz butter

8 dessert spoons brandy

Tart Tatin

50 g/ 2 oz butter

75 g/ 3 oz/ ³/₄ cup caster sugar

4 medium-sized peeled red onions

4 pieces of puff pastry cut into 12–14 cm. (5 in.) diameter disks, each 4 mm. (¹/₄ in.) thick

To Serve

100 g/ 4 oz/ ¹/₂ cup soured cream with chopped chives

1 bunch watercress, washed, larger stalks discarded

Begin by making the tart tatins. Melt the butter in a large, non-stick ovenproof frying pan over a medium heat. Add the sugar and season. Cook slowly until the sugar has started to caramelise. Slice 1 cm. (¹/₂ in.) off the top of the red onions, place the flat surface of each one onto the pan and cook for 1 minute. Carefully cover the onions with the pastry disks and place in the oven for 50 minutes. When cooked, the pastry will be golden brown and the onion should be very soft and sweet.

Heat some oil in a large frying pan. Press the peppercorns onto both sides of the steaks and season with salt, then brown on both sides. Add the knob of butter to the pan and continue cooking until the meat is cooked to your liking. Remove the steaks from the pan, add the brandy to the juices and cook for 30 seconds in order to burn off the alcohol.

Divide the pan juices between the steaks and serve with the warm onion tarts, sour cream and watercress.

The bull was the religious sacrificial animal par excellence in the Classical Mediterranean world. This Roman marble head, circa 2nd Century A.D., was once perhaps part of a column capital supporting the roof of a temple in Asia Minor. It was sold in New York in December 2004 for $18,000 (£9,419)

Table Settings

The decoration of the table has changed as dining habits have altered over time. Formerly in the large dining room of the Palazzo of the Princes d'Avalos in Naples, this large gilt *surtout de table* by Thomire was sold by Sotheby's for £310,000 ($512,120) in 2003 and can now be seen in the Rothschild Collection at Waddesdon Manor in Buckinghamshire

Simon Thurley, Chief Executive of English Heritage; Sara Paston-Williams, historic food advisor to the National Trust; interior designer, Melissa Wyndham; Matthew Dennison, Fine Arts Editor, House & Garden; and Mario Tavella, head of the Furniture division Sotheby's Europe, discuss the development of the dining room and the impact of changing habits

Mario Tavella: My area of specialisation is based upon the decorative arts of dining but I wondered if anyone could shed some light on the origin of the dining room itself?

Sara Paston-Williams: As far as I am aware, dining rooms grew out of the medieval great halls, and a desire by those with wealth and power for more privacy and for the family to dine without being under the gaze of their retinue and servants.

MT: So from the very start it was a separate room rather than an area being cordoned off?

SPW: They started with a reserved area, and then began to build specific spaces and ultimately constructed a private room, away from the communal dining hall. This really gave a different feel to the whole process: they chose to eat in a more secluded manner with their family or with invited guests, which made it more of an occasion.

Matthew Dennison: It is part of a general movement towards greater intimacy in the home. It's not simply about eating.

MT: So having a dining room has always been something aspirational for those outside of the upper classes then.

Simon Thurley: In fact, in Britain the dining room as we would recognise it – set up exclusively for meals – does not really exist until about 1740, which is surprisingly recent. Prior to that people would have moved around the house.

Melissa Wyndham: People set up dining rooms when they needed to and otherwise used the room for other things, which I think began in France and is something that they still do.

MD: In French country houses, tables are still sometimes brought out and set up in a room for a particular meal.

ST: It is actually a nice thing to do. If you look at somewhere like Ham House in West London, which dates from the mid-17th century, there is not a dining room in that house. There's no great hall and no single dining room. They would have set things up

and removed them when the space was not in use and often they would have been normal rooms.

SPW: There were rooms that were regularly used for dining though aren't there?

ST: Well, there were a couple of rooms that would have been used regularly but no permanent dining room furniture. It's difficult to pinpoint specifically when the first room was made as a dining room but one of the earliest was Sir Robert Walpole's house, Houghton Hall. The increased desire for privacy was in parallel with an increased specialisation in the use of rooms. Before the actual dining room, separate elements of a meal eaten in different parts of the house.

MD: In a number of 17th-century houses, the meal would end on the roof, where guests moved to eat dessert in special rooftop pavilions.

MT: The furniture prior to 1740 reflects this too – the tables were large and heavy wooden pieces, obviously created for several uses other than simply eating.

ST: Furniture of this sort had much lower status then as well, if you had a table you would cover it. All the things that appeal to us about those pieces now – the grain and finish beautiful oak and elm wood – was the last thing the original owners would have shown off.

MW: You mentioned 1740 earlier – that seems a very exact date for the start of the dining room.

ST: Well, the first room I know of that was specially designed as a dining room, was built for Queen Anne at Hampton Court Palace between 1710 and 1740. It was a room specifically called a public dining room and was actually built for eating in, unlike other houses of the time, which had salons that could be used for numerous things besides dining. I think it was due to social life operating in a more formalised and structured way. It returns to those two themes we have already mentioned: privacy and room specialisation come together. Another factor is servants and how they communicated with them, so often the kitchen needed to be next door to where they were eating.

MW: Although later they were often very far apart weren't they?

ST: Absolutely, which I think was due to the invention of the bell pull and later, in the 19th century, the electric bell. It suddenly allowed the kitchen to be placed at a distance.

SPW: The kitchen at Petworth in West Sussex was miles away, under a tunnel or something

MT: In Lucca, at Villa Pecci-Blunt, the kitchen is linked to the dining room by a small train. It was so important to have the kitchen at a distance.

ST: For two reasons. Smell and fire – even after the introduction of coal grates, which contained the fire more effectively, the risks to a great house of fire were enormous.

MD: At Osborne, Queen Victoria's house on the Isle of Wight, which was started in the 1840s, the kitchen is in the service wing, well detached from the main body of the house.

ST: That is one of the reasons the rich would be served in silver, because it is such a fantastic insulator. In my view, it is a myth that everything in these houses was freezing cold because of the distance from the kitchen. A proper silver tureen is the most perfect insulator.

SPW: The domes covering food also helped and plates were kept warm using hot water. Many ways of heating food were devised – there's an amazing metal plate warmer at Kedleston Hall in Derbyshire, which was designed to stand in front of the fire.

MT: Did changes to what people ate and how they ate effect how the food was served at the table?

SPW: I think it was due to the French influence, and prior to that the food had been more openly displayed on the table, so the attractiveness of the food – rather than the dishes themselves – was part of the experience of the meal.

ST: Also in the 16th and early 17th century, meals were much closer to what we would call a buffet, where tables were covered with many dishes and people took what they wanted. Eating, as today, was all to do with status – where you sat, who served you, what you ate from, the number of courses was of tremendous importance as it denoted social rank. People were anxious about eating in the proper fashion.

MT: I suppose elements of that come into why people buy and use silver today. I am sure that many people who buy at auction use the pieces – and I hope that they do because these pieces are designed to be enjoyed doing what they were made for. We had a splendid gilt bronze *surtout de table*, which was one of the largest ever, and we sold it to Waddesdon Manor, the Rothschild House in Buckinghamshire, now owned by the National Trust, and they use it for formal dinners. It measures about four metres and looks wonderful filled with flowers.

MW: That's interesting because sometimes, decoratively speaking, the dining room was the most boring room in the house.

MD: There's an interesting divide between great houses and lesser houses, with much more of a gender association for middle-class dining rooms than those in so-called 'great' houses.

ST: The gender aspect is a really important point. A dining room is a masculine room, with dark furniture and hangings and it was often the place where family portraits were displayed. After dinner the ladies withdrew to a lighter room with lighter furniture, which really emphasises the gender differences.

SPW: Mario, did the European dining room develop along similar lines?

MT: No, I wouldn't say so. There are some wonderful collections of objects such as Sèvres porcelain, which were often kept simply for display. There also seem to be fewer large dining tables, and, while the British developed specific pieces for the dining room, like the sideboard, the French and Italian tradition was to have more consoles in the dining room.

MD: Robert Adam said in the 1770s, that the French spent much less time eating than the English did so they gave less thought to their dining rooms.

ST: Mentioning sideboards is interesting because I think there is a long pedigree for pieces like this in England. It starts with that idea of medieval meals almost taking the form of a buffet, and the opportunity to display your plates continues through Tudor dining rooms right down to the sideboard of the 19th and 20th centuries. Even if you weren't using your best soup tureen, you'd have it on the sideboard so at least everyone knows you have one.

MD: There's a story from the beginning of the last century about the great rivalry between the Duchess of Devonshire and the Duchess of Portland over their silver collections. Whenever they went to dinner they got a little bit more out until the Duchess of Portland had everything on display and the Duchess of Devonshire said to her after their meal: 'Your table looks wonderful, after dinner you must take me to see the vaults'.

ST: Looking after a collection like that would be a full-time job, which relates to another element that effects dining habits. The

An increasingly prevalent alternative to a large dining room table is to lay a smaller one in a window to allow for a more intimate atmosphere. This example was from the collection of renowned furniture dealer Christopher Hodsoll, which sold for £1,101,096 ($1,716,976) in London in 2002

issue of servants: first they are moved down into the basement and the introduction of back stairs and back rooms meant they were never seen. Ultimately though servants vanish, and all the elements that they provided for formal dining vanish. What is left is how people dine today, which doesn't really involve a dining room at all.

MW: I am asked repeatedly to build a family room, which is essentially demolishing the wall between the dining room and kitchen. It puts everything together in one room and everything is done there, from cooking and eating to watching television. It is no longer a priority to have a dining room.

MT: I agree. Consequently though there is a real sense of those traditional pieces of brown furniture becoming unfashionable, which seems such a shame as they are often stunning pieces that might work in another room or context just as well.

SPW: What makes a good dining room if you're creating one?

MW: To my mind the lighting is vital and must be subtle, candlelight is by far the best. The room must not be noisy. Fabric or tapestries absorb sound, otherwise you can't hear anything when you are eating. The room must be interesting visually – and finally of course good food is essential.

MT: Recently I have seen more houses that use one or two small tables, or a few tables in different rooms.

MW: That's a charming idea. When you don't always have large dinners, you place a breakfast table in a dining room, perhaps in the window, so you don't have to sit two people at a large table.

ST: It is interesting to think about what might be next for dining and dining rooms. We've reached this terrible situation where everyone is eating in their kitchens and, as fashions constantly change, it will be interesting to see what happens next. Hopefully there will be a revival in building dining rooms as people realise that formality and theatre around presenting a meal is actually an extremely elegant thing to do.

SPW: Another alternative is people choosing which of the formal elements they want to include, so perhaps drinks or a starter somewhere and then eating in the kitchen. It means that one of the party is not isolated, which relates back to the point about servants. Now, someone has to be in the kitchen and it is often the host. I think that formal elements can be adapted to a relaxed atmosphere.

MD: Formal entertaining makes great demands on the host, if the host is also the cook. For any but the most accomplished cook, the pressures of formal dining can be extremely unrelaxing.

ST: I think it's time for a revival of formal dining and the dining room. My view is that dining is like theatre. I think it's really wonderful to have drinks in one room and then open the doors to the dining room and hear people catch their breath. I love that sense of theatre – the wonderful cutlery and crockery, the starched linen, the candelabra and the room flickering with candlelight, and you close the door, the fire's raging and there's a buzz of conversation and expectation. The whole room works together like an incredible stage set with a performance about to take place.

This banana dessert is easier to make than the classic apple tart tatin and delicious when topped with vanilla ice cream

BANANA TART TATIN WITH VANILLA ICE CREAM

Serves 4 • Preparation time: 15 minutes • Cooking time: 15 minutes • Pre-heat oven to 220 °C/ 425 °F/ gas-mark 7

Banana Tart Tatin

1 disk of puff pastry, 22 cm. (9 in.) diameter and 5 mm. (¼ in.) thick

100 g/ 4 oz/ 1 cup caster sugar

3 bananas, sliced at an angle

To Serve

Vanilla ice cream (page 157)

Prepare the vanilla ice cream beforehand (page 157). Cook the puff pastry on an oven tray for 8 minutes until risen and golden.

Heat the sugar in a 22 cm. (9 in.) ovenproof frying pan and stir with a wooden spoon until caramelised. Add the bananas to the caramel, arranging them evenly over the base of the pan. Cover with the puff pastry and cook in the oven for 5 minutes.

Turn the tart out onto a serving plate, cut into quarters and serve with the vanilla ice cream.

This traditional pudding is delicious when prepared with richer breads like brioche, croissant or panettone

White & Dark Chocolate Bread & Butter Pudding

Serves 4–6 • Preparation time: 15 minutes • Cooking time: 30 minutes • Pre-heat oven to 170 °C/ 325 °F/ gas-mark 3

300 ml/ ½ pint/ 1¼ cups milk

300 ml/ ½ pint/ 1¼ cups double cream

1 vanilla pod, split and deseeded

2 whole eggs

2 egg yolks

75 g/ 3 oz/ ¾ cup caster sugar

4 croissants, sliced open

75 g/ 3 oz/ ¾ cup white chocolate

75 g/ 3 oz/ ¾ cup dark chocolate

To Serve

Icing sugar

Cream or vanilla ice cream (page 157)

If serving with vanilla ice cream, be sure to prepare this in advance (page 157). Simmer the milk, cream and vanilla pod. Whisk the eggs, yolks and sugar until blended and pour over the milk and cream, mixing all the time. Strain the mixture. Place half of the croissants in a layer on the bottom of a buttered ovenproof dish, then sprinkle half of the white and dark chocolate over them and pour over half of the egg and cream mixture. Repeat the process, pressing down the croissants so they absorb the mix. Cook for 30 minutes. The custard should be slightly soft in the middle.

Dust with icing sugar and serve with cream or vanilla ice cream.

Executed in 1962 during the penultimate year of Piero Manzoni's tragically short life, Achrome, which sold for $464,000 (£249,622) in New York in May 2006, is the second largest of only 13 works he made using Italian bread 'rosettes' or panini and kaolin on panel

This simple, yet hearty, pudding is a wonderful combination of flavours, colours and textures

RICE PUDDING, POACHED RHUBARB & LEMON CURD

Serves 4 • Preparation time: 15 minutes • Cooking time: 1 hour • Pre-heat oven to 170 °C/ 325 °F/ gas-mark 3

Pudding

50 g/ 2 oz/ ¹⁄₃ cup pudding rice

4 level dessert spoons caster sugar

300 ml/ ¹⁄₂ pint/ 1¹⁄₄ cups milk

300 ml/ ¹⁄₂ pint/ 1¹⁄₄ cups double cream

¹⁄₂ vanilla pod, split down the middle and deseeded

¹⁄₄ tsp freshly grated nutmeg

25 g/ 1 oz unsalted butter

Rhubarb

275 g/ 10 oz rhubarb, washed and trimmed to 7 cm. (3 in.) sticks

75 g/ 3 oz/ ¹⁄₃ cup caster sugar

To Serve

Lemon curd (page 156)

First make the lemon curd (page 156). For the pudding, mix all the ingredients in a pan and bring to simmering point, stirring occasionally. Transfer to an ovenproof dish and cook for 45 minutes until the rice is soft. Place the rhubarb in a single layer on an oven tray, sprinkle over the sugar and cover with foil. Cook at the same temperature as the rice pudding for 20 minutes or until the rhubarb is soft, but still holds its shape. Take out and cool. Set aside the pudding for 15 minutes before serving.

Arrange the rhubarb with its juices to one side, the rice pudding to the other, and spoon over the lemon curd.

WINE THROUGH THE SEASONS

WINTER

by Serena Sutcliffe MW

Winter is when the vines slumber and the wines in the cellar settle down and start their maturation process. Snow can look lovely in vineyards, powdering the stark outline of the vines and making them gleam, but it can also protect them from the ravages of frost, forming a blanket cover of relative warmth. Really cold temperatures are dangerous, but less so in the depths of winter when the vines are 'hibernating'. However, a real winter freeze, such as that suffered in St Emilion and Pomerol in 1956, can wreak devastation and kill thousands of vines. Some varieties are more resistant to extreme cold than others, Chardonnay and Riesling being more hardy than Pinot Noir or Cabernet Sauvignon. You can really shiver in the vineyards of Germany, Austria and Switzerland, while the snow coverage of the vines at Massandra in the Crimea can be dramatic.

All is not asleep, however. Pruning takes place in winter, usually after the first frost has caused the leaves to fall, exposing the canes. The aim of pruning is to control the yield in the vineyard, which ultimately affects quality – less normally means better in this instance. Pruning also determines the shape of the vine, making other vineyard manoeuvres easier and preventing the vines from spreading between the rows. The type of pruning is dictated by tradition, or regional laws, and it can continue throughout the winter. It is a very cold task, agony for the fingers, demanding experience as well as endurance. For the onlooker, the scene is timeless, with wafts of smoke emerging from the burning excess wood, almost Brueghel-like had there been vines in Flanders!

In the cellar, the wine begins its maturation, which can be over years, or months in the case of fresh white wine designed for young drinking. It is also the time for blending, or *assemblage,* as it is known in French wine regions, notably in Bordeaux, where the principal grape varieties and different plots in the vineyards are blended together, according to quality, to make the first *grand vin* and then the second wine. In Champagne, the art of the blender is one of the most exacting exercises in all winemaking, composing the *cuvées* out of two or three grape varieties and myriad villages and sites. The process is also vital in the creation of great Vintage Port and fine Sherry, with the mosaic of all the component parts then learning to live with each other as the wines age.

Perhaps the very best winter activity is consuming one's most precious red wines, and lingering over venerable Madeira and Port, the cold, inhospitable weather being most conducive to the appreciation of bottles with gravitas!

The wine maturing in casks in the first year cellar at Château Haut-Brion

Spring

In the 1880s, when Georges Seurat spent two years painting his most famous work, *Un Dimanche Après-Midi à L'Ile de la Grande Jatte*, he captured this popular recreation place on the Seine. Exemplifying his Pointillist style, this painting, which sold at Sotheby's New York in 1999 from the collection of Mr and Mrs John Hay Whitney for $35,202,500 (£21,473,525), is one of the numerous preparatory works for his famous painting of the scene

Courgette flowers can be hard to find, but they are so striking, that they are well worth the hunt

LEMON RICOTTA STUFFED COURGETTE FLOWERS, MIZUNA & TARRAGON DRESSING

Serves 4 • Preparation time: 25 minutes • Cooking time: 6 minutes • Pre-heat oil to 180 °C/ 350 °F

175 g/ 6 oz/ ¾ cup ricotta cheese

1 heaped tsp lemon zest

2 tsp lemon juice

1 heaped dessert spoon roughly chopped basil

2 dessert spoons grated Parmesan

4 sun-dried tomatoes, roughly chopped

A few chilli flakes (optional)

4 courgette flowers, with courgettes attached

1 litre/ 36 fl oz/ 4 cups vegetable oil
for deep frying

Beer batter (page 154)

To Serve

50 g/ 2 oz washed mizuna leaves

Tarragon dressing (page 153)

Prepare the batter (page 154) and the tarragon dressing (page 153). In a bowl, thoroughly mix the ricotta, lemon zest and juice, basil, Parmesan, sun-dried tomatoes and chilli flakes and lightly season. Gently open the courgette flowers, remove the stamen and divide the ricotta mixture between them. Close the flowers, ensure the ricotta mix is completely enclosed and twist the tops to secure them.

Preheat the oil in a deep fat fryer. Dip the whole courgette and flower into the batter and place into the oil. Fry for 5–6 minutes until it is golden on both sides and then take out and drain on kitchen paper. Repeat this process with each courgette flower.

Dress the mizuna leaves with tarragon dressing and serve with one flower to the side.

Salads are extremely popular in the Cafe and this classic example is perhaps the most sought after. It easily doubles as a main course

SMOKED CHICKEN WALDORF SALAD

Serves 4 • Preparation time: 30 minutes

150 ml/ ¼ pint/ ⅔ cup lemon aioli (page 150)

175 g/ 6 oz sliced smoked chicken

2 baby gem lettuce leaves, separated and washed

25 g/ 1 oz walnuts

1 celery stick, finely sliced

½ Cox's apple, cored and finely sliced

½ bunch chives, cut into 1 cm. (½ in.) batons

Prepare the lemon aioli (page 150). Mix all of the ingredients except the chives in a bowl and toss with the aioli.

Place the salad onto serving plates and sprinkle with the chives. Serve with fresh, crusty bread.

One of the last great relics of the American Revolution, this silk regimental colour flag from circa 1776 is, the first recorded with 13 alternating red and white stripes and was auctioned for $12,336,000 (£6,703,911) in an unprecedented sale for Sotheby's New York in 2006

This is delicious for brunch. When in season, blood oranges make the perfect Maltaise sauce

Asparagus, Smoked Salmon, Poached Egg & Maltaise Sauce

Serves 4 • Preparation time: 30 minutes • Cooking time: 10 minutes

4 eggs

20 cooked asparagus spears

175 g/ 6 oz sliced smoked salmon

Sea salt and freshly ground black pepper

Maltaise sauce (page 151)

Prepare the Maltaise sauce (page 151) and lightly poach the eggs.

Divide the asparagus and salmon between serving plates and place the egg on top of the salmon. Sprinkle sea salt and pepper over the egg and spoon over the Maltaise sauce.

Traditionally the chicken is cooked entirely in the pot, but by browning the skin first, more colour is added to the finished dish

GUINEA FOWL POT-AU-FEU WITH SPRING VEGETABLES & TARRAGON DUMPLINGS

Serves 4 • Preparation time: 1 hour • Cooking time: 30 minutes

Pot-au-Feu

4 guinea fowl breasts

600 ml/ 1 pint/ 2¹/₂ cups chicken stock (page 154)

Spring Vegetables

12 baby carrots, cooked and peeled

50 g/ 2 oz garden peas, lightly blanched

8 spring onions, trimmed and lightly blanched

Dumplings

50 g/ 2 oz/ ¹/₂ cup self-raising flour

50 g/ 2 oz/ ¹/₂ cup ground almonds

1 heaped dessert spoon finely chopped tarragon

2 egg yolks

25 g/ 1 oz melted unsalted butter

25 ml/ 1 fl oz/ ¹/₈ cup boiling water

2 large pinches of salt and pepper

First make the chicken stock (page 154). For the dumplings, mix the flour, almonds and tarragon in a bowl. Then add the egg yolks, butter, boiling water, salt and pepper and mix to a paste. Roll into 16 small balls and drop into a large pan of lightly salted boiling water. Simmer for 15–20 minutes and remove with a slotted spoon.

Season and cook the guinea fowl breasts in a frying pan with a little oil until they are brown on both sides. Transfer them to the re-heated chicken stock and simmer for about 15 minutes until cooked. Just before serving, add the spring vegetables and dumplings and heat through, then divide between large soup bowls.

VEAL T-BONE

WITH A SALAD OF FRENCH BEANS,
NEW POTATOES & WHITE BEAN ROUILLE

Serves 4 • Preparation time: 45 minutes • Cooking time: 20 minutes
• Pre-heat oven to 200 °C/ 400 °F/ gas-mark 6

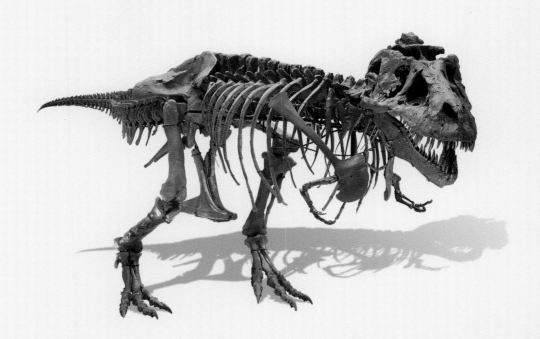

This combination of regional flavours is easy to prepare and makes a wonderfully light main course

4 veal T-bone chops, 175 g/ 6 oz each

Salad

1 radicchio, quartered and stem removed

225 g/ 8 oz new potatoes, boiled and sliced

50 g/ 2 oz/ ¹⁄₃ cup Calamata olives

225 g/ 8 oz French beans, trimmed and cooked

Rouille

2 garlic cloves, skin on

100 g/ 4 oz/ ²⁄₃ cup cooked cannelini beans,
and cooking liquor

120 ml/ 4 fl oz/ ¹⁄₂ cup lemon oil (page 153)

1 dessert spoon lemon juice

Splash of Tabasco

First prepare the lemon oil (page 153). Place the radicchio and garlic on an oven tray, drizzle with a little olive oil and season. Cook for 12 minutes until softened. Separate the radicchio leaves and set aside.

For the rouille, squeeze the garlic cloves out of their skins, place in a food processor with the cooked cannelini beans and 4 dessert spoons of their cooking liquid, half of the lemon oil, the lemon juice and Tabasco. Process until smooth and season to taste.

Heat a large frying pan and brown the seasoned chops on both sides in vegetable oil. Place in the oven and cook for 8–10 minutes.

To make the salad, mix the new potatoes, radicchio, olives and French beans together in a bowl. Dress with the remaining lemon oil. Divide between serving plates, place the chops to the side and spoon over the rouille.

One of the most extraordinary items ever offered for auction passed through Sotheby's New York in 1997: 'Sue', the largest and most complete fossilized skeleton of a Tyrannosaurus Rex sold for $8,362,500 (£5,184,750) now resides in the Field Museum of Natural History in Chicago

This unusual combination of ingredients creates a stunning dish. The tuna is also delicious when cooked on a barbecue

Seared Tuna with Broad Bean, Avocado & Watermelon Salad

Serves 4 • Preparation time: 30 minutes • Cooking time: 5 minutes • Pre-heat the char-grill pan 10 minutes before use

4 tuna steaks, 175 g/ 6 oz each

Salad

1 large avocado

175 g/ 6 oz/ 1 cup cooked cannelini beans

100 g/ 4 oz/ ³/₄ cup broad beans, cooked with white skin removed

175 g/ 6 oz/ 1 cup watermelon, cut into 1.5 cm. (⁵/₈ in.) cubes

Lime dressing (page 153)

To Serve

A few sprigs of coriander

First make the lime dressing (page 153).

Peel the avocado and cut into 1 cm. (¹/₂ in.) chunks, add the cannelini beans, broad beans and watermelon, pour over the dressing and season.

Rub some vegetable oil over both sides of the tuna steaks and season well. When the char-grill pan is hot, cook the steaks on each side for 1 minute or until char-grill marks have formed.

Divide the dressed salad onto four plates, cut the tuna in half at an angle, place on top of the salad and garnish with coriander.

Rufino Tamayo's Sandías (Fette d'Anguria) from 1958 depicts one of his best known icons, the watermelon, which is a staple of the Mexican diet and symbolic of the artist's patriotism. The painting was sold for $1,215,750 (£851,025) in the Latin American Art sale in New York in November 2000

Roast Mediterranean Vegetables with Sage & Parmesan Polenta & Hazelnut Butter

Serves 4 • Preparation time: 45 minutes • Cooking time: 1 hour
• Pre-heat oven to 200 °C/ 400 °F/ gas-mark 6 • Pre-heat char-grill 10 minutes before use

As the Cafe is a lunch-time venue, a vegetarian dish like this is popular for those seeking a lighter alternative

Roast Vegetables

1 aubergine, thickly sliced

2 red onions, peeled and quartered

2 Romano peppers

2 courgettes, thickly sliced diagonally

Polenta

475 ml/ 16 fl oz/ 2 cups water

75 g/ 3 oz/ 1 cup polenta

1 heaped dessert spoon chopped sage

50 g/ 2 oz butter

75 g/ 3 oz/ ³/₄ cup grated Parmesan

Dash of cream

Hazelnut Butter

50 g/ 2 oz unsalted butter

25 g/ 1 oz roasted hazelnuts, lightly crushed

To Serve

8 large basil leaves

100 ml/ 3¹/₂ fl oz/ ¹/₂ cup balsamic vinegar

First make the balsamic syrup with which the dish is served. Pour the balsamic vinegar into a pan, place over a high heat and bring to the boil, then reduce by three quarters and leave to cool.

Put all of the vegetables, apart from the courgettes on separate trays, season well and drizzle with olive oil. Cook the aubergine and onions in the oven until soft. Roast the peppers, put them in a bowl and cover with cling film, leave to cool before peeling off the skins and removing the seeds and stalks. Season and char-grill the courgettes on both sides. Allow all of the vegetables to cool.

Bring the water to the boil and steadily pour in the polenta, stirring all the time. Lower the heat, cover and cook for 3–5 minutes. When cooked, stir in the sage, butter, Parmesan, cream and season generously. Keep warm.

Melt the unsalted butter and cook over a medium heat until it starts to turn golden brown, remove from heat and add the hazelnuts and a pinch of salt.

Spoon the polenta onto plates and arrange the vegetables around it. Garnish with the hazelnut butter and torn basil leaves and finish by drizzling with the balsamic syrup.

Cecil Beaton's images of Daisy Fellowes encapsulate the glamour and style of her world. Both of these photographs show her wearing the Cartier 'tutti frutti' necklace, as part of an exotic fancy dress costume for the famous Beistegui Ball in 1961 (above), and in a more formal portrait (right)

PR: I believe Louis Cartier had already begun to think about new and innovative styles at the start of the century. That was one reason he introduced platinum into their jewels, as it was less dazzling when seen in the newly installed electric lights that were everywhere. He also sought inspiration from other sources, going back to designs from the 18th century – but with platinum it was totally new. This showed how his mind worked and he found inspiration in Cubism, in the *ballets russe*. I think the pieces now known as Art Deco were really born 20 years before, we have brooches from then that are totally symmetrical and geometrical.

GG: So exotic designs such as the 'tutti frutti' were a move against that?

PR: Perhaps more of a development from. Nothing totally replaces that which went before it, as you know. I'm not sure if there was any definite closure between one era and the next.

GG: I've just finished shooting jewellery for the autumn/ winter issues of *Harper's Bazaar*. Pierre, in terms of jewellery design, do you think it remains possible to pursue the exotic today?

PR: That is a very interesting question. Exoticism isn't the same now as it was in the 1920s and 30s because now people have the occasion to travel and see so many different things, which has influenced the evolution of ethnic style jewellery. Then the interest for exotic items was more exclusive, as only a minority had access to travel – now it is a totally different situation. At Cartier we are still influenced by Indian style for example, and still work with emeralds and rubies, but the structure of modern jewellery is very light, which is different from earlier pieces. A 'tutti frutti' necklace today has a totally different feel to that of 70 years ago. Women today don't dress the same or have the same body shape – or even the same role in society – and don't wear the same jewellery.

GG: I also think that colour is particularly exotic now – the use of semi-precious stones adds a lot of colour and mood, which relates to Cartier's historical use of colour in their jewellery. Modern jewellery also comes in a range of prices meaning this style is available to a wider variety of people. Fashion has a huge amount of influence on how people perceive jewellery: what they wear and how they display it is now more mass-market than it use to be. It used to be elitist and people would show off their wealth by their jewellery. Now they are also spending on shoes, bags and clothes, and jewellery has become wrapped up with that.

AR: There is definitely something in that. The way that people buy and wear jewels has evolved – reflecting the changing position of women in society – but high-end jewellery, the unique pieces, they will always remain important and desirable.

PR: When you wear unique pieces, it feels as though you are wearing a work of art. People feel differently about more everyday pieces. There remains a difference between day and evening jewellery and how those pieces are worn. Social life has changed – during the day you see more people when you go out. Socialites from the 1930s to the 1960s didn't meet as many people and tended to meet within their circle of friends. Now you meet people, at work, in the street or shopping – and need a variety of jewellery.

GG: I think society and celebrity was entirely different then, a more closed and tight community. Now the effect a celebrity, a famous actress or even a painter has is immense in terms of the inspiration they provide. People are more inclined to look up to people with talent, as opposed to their position in society, and reflect that in the styles and jewels they wear.

PR: There is something liberating in this new freedom to express oneself through jewellery– in exactly the same way that Daisy Fellowes did. The artistic value of jewellery is more recognised and women feel more free to chose original pieces that express their personality and are really strong in terms of design.

AR: I think, in addition to going to retailers such as Cartier, people are attracted to auction for such pieces. The Daisy Fellowes' necklace we sold in Geneva is a prime example, but more modern pieces as well. Another trend we have noticed is people buying stones that they then have set, which means they are more involved in the process of designing their pieces. In this sense it is exactly the same as how women like the Duchess of Windsor or Daisy Fellowes worked with Cartier: working alongside a jewellery designer to create a piece that was a reflection of their character.

PR: Daisy Fellowes importance should not be underestimated in this respect – her boldness and daring meant that important pieces such as the 'tutti frutti' necklace came into being and continue to be influential.

AR: I think another great thing about her was, through her love of travel, she would go to such places as India and choose the stones that she then had made into jewellery. While people still do that, I think it would be difficult to become so influential today.

PR: I think perhaps now some of the real arbiters of taste buy older, more important pieces, and remain relatively unknown, because they want to be private. Daisy Fellowes was open and public about the pieces she was buying.

AR: It's interesting to think about what constitutes a classic today, something that is really timeless and a wonderful work of art. Working in the auction world, a great deal of emphasis is placed on the major Impressionist paintings and I always feel something like the 'tutti frutti' pieces are the equivalent masterpieces in the jewellery world.

GG: I think some of the newer collections will become icons too – something like the Cartier Orchid Collection will go on to become a classic I believe. I think people will continue to want to own it and it will still be as beautiful and desired in 20 or 50 years as it is now.

AR: I wonder if, as in the social world that Daisy Fellowes once inhabited, lunch remains an important institution?

GG: I think in certain areas of society and definitely for work. Especially my work life in magazines, lunch is incredibly important. It's where a great deal of networking is done and contacts established, and is a relaxed atmosphere, where getting to know someone is much easier and certainly more informal.

AR: I think it is the same in the auction world as well. I find it the perfect occasion to get to know people more intimately and discuss their tastes in art and especially jewellery.

GG: I think there is a real distinction between a working lunch and a more social lunch. I went with some colleagues to a big fashion lunch recently, all dressed for business and at the same event were these beautiful women, impeccably dressed because the lunch was more of a social event for them.

PR: I agree. Lunchtime is almost a luxury time. If you really have a good lunch in a good place, it is a statement that you can afford this much time. When I get invited to one of these lunches, in Paris or a private club in New York, you see how elegantly dressed everyone is and you have the feeling of being privileged. When you think of it, a lunchtime like that is very special.

GG: I think there is also a trend among people to have breakfast meetings, which is quite a new development. Many restaurants in London now open at nine or earlier. It's perfect, you go to the office and then out to a breakfast meeting, which you can even follow with a lunch if you want to.

AR: Who would be your ideal lunch partners?

PR: There are many of our clients at Cartier who I love as lunch partners. My dream lunch would be to talk to Elizabeth Taylor about jewellery and, for a conversation as interesting as that I would have no trouble leaving the choice of where we ate up to her.

AR: That would be wonderful, I think I would like to take a place at that table.

GG: I could always make up the four – I think any more than four is too many.

AR: Another fascinating table would be lunch at Sotheby's Cafe – with Daisy Fellowes herself of course.

According to Eton lore, a group of schoolboys dropped their hamper while going on a picnic, mixing the meringue, cream and berries and creating this dish

ETON MESS WITH HAZELNUT CRUNCH

Serves 4–6 • Preparation time: 10 minutes • Cooking time: 1 hour • Pre-heat oven to 110 °C/ 225 °F/ gas-mark ¼

Meringue

100 ml/ 3½ fl oz/ ½ cup egg whites

150 g/ 6 oz/ 1½ cups caster sugar

Hazelnut Crunch

75 g/ 3 oz/ ⅓ cup caster sugar

25 g/ 1 oz/ ¼ cup hazelnuts

To Serve

250 ml/ 9 fl oz/ 1 cup double cream, lightly whipped

300 g/ 11 oz fresh mixed red berries

Begin by making the meringue: whisk the egg whites until firm, add half of the sugar and whisk again until it forms stiff peaks. Transfer to a large bowl, sprinkle over the remaining sugar and fold-in with a large, metal spoon. Line an oven tray with baking parchment and spoon on the meringue. Flatten to a smooth surface and place in the oven for 1 hour or until the meringue is light brown.

For the hazelnut crunch, put the sugar in a heavy-bottomed saucepan over a medium heat. Stir with a wooden spoon until caramelised, drop in the hazelnuts and coat thoroughly with the caramel. Pour the mix onto an oiled tray and allow to set. Once cool, break into pieces with a rolling pin or crumble in a food processor.

Break up the meringue in a large bowl, add the whipped cream and berries and stir. Place in serving dishes and sprinkle with hazelnut crunch.

Champagne & Alphonso Mango Jelly with Mango Cream

Serves 5 • Preparation time: 45 minutes • Setting time: 2 hours

The champagne and mangoes are delicate but effective in this colourful dish. The mango season is short, but the dessert is also wonderful with summer berries

Jelly

140 g/ 5 oz/ 1 cup caster sugar

160 ml/ 5¹/₂ fl oz/ ²/₃ cup water

400 ml/ 14 fl oz/ 1³/₄ cups champagne

5 gelatine leaves

150 g/ 5 oz Alphonso mango, cut into 1 cm. (¹/₂ in.) cubes

Mango Cream

100 g/ 3 oz/ 1 cup puréed Alphonso mango

175 ml/ 6 fl oz/ ³/₄ cup double cream, lightly whipped

1 dessert spoon caster sugar

Make the sugar syrup by heating the sugar and water in a pan and boiling for 2 minutes. Add the champagne and take off the heat. Put the gelatine leaves in cold water until softened, then remove and squeeze well. Stir the gelatine into the champagne mix until completely dissolved, place the liquid in the fridge and check regularly to see if it has started to set. When the jelly is slightly wobbly, stir in the mango cubes. Divide between five ramekins and leave them in the fridge to set fully, it should take around 2 hours.

To make the cream, mix the puréed mango, cream and sugar together and chill until ready to serve.

Have a saucepan of hot water ready, dip the moulds into the water for a few seconds, then tip them out onto serving plates and garnish with mango cream.

This is a dessert for chocolate lovers and is most striking when served in tall, thin glasses to display the layers. Decorate it with a glacé cherry for the ultimate classic look

Trio of Chocolate

Serves 4 • Preparation time: 45 minutes • Cooling time: 3 hours

450 ml/ ³/₄ pint/ 1³/₄cups double cream

1¹/₂ vanilla pods, deseeded

8 egg yolks

75 g/ 3 oz/ ¹/₂ cup caster sugar

40 g/ 1¹/₂ oz dark chocolate

40 g/ 1¹/₂ oz milk chocolate

40 g/ 1¹/₂ oz white chocolate

Bring the cream and vanilla pods to simmering point, then remove from heat. Whisk the egg yolks and sugar together. Pour the cream into the egg mix, whisking all the time. Return to a clean saucepan, stir over a moderate heat, without boiling, until the mixture has thickened into a custard, then strain.

Melt the dark, milk and white chocolates separately. Add a third of the custard to each and mix thoroughly. Then, starting with the dark chocolate mixture, divide between four champagne glasses and chill for 1 hour. Repeat this process with the milk, then the white chocolate, making three distinct layers of colour. Remove from the fridge 1 hour before serving.

Vik Muniz rendered this seminal photograph of Jackson Pollock painting in Bosco chocolate syrup. From his Pictures of Chocolate series, it sold for $78,000 (£46,039) at the Contemporary Art sale in New York in November 2003 to the Collection of Peter Marino N.Y.

WINE THROUGH THE SEASONS

SPRING

by Serena Sutcliffe MW

The earth springs into life at this time, full of promise and burgeoning buds, heralding the start of the new growing season in the vineyard. Budbreak gives us the first glimpse of green, as the young leaves emerge from the buds. This is the moment when a spring frost could do damage so all eyes are on the weather forecasts. 'Spring' usually means budding in March in the northern hemisphere, but September for the southern hemisphere. Other vineyard operations involve shoot thinning to reduce leaf density, and shoot positioning which facilitates vineyard work right up to the harvest and helps control diseases and pests in an ecological way. Any planting of new vineyards is done in early spring.

Meanwhile, much will be going on in the cellar. There will be bottling for six-month old wines that are sold young and fresh, such as light Sauvignons, white wines from the Mâconnais and Gamay wines from the Beaujolais, as well as simple *vins de pays* and their equivalents from the New World. Serious wines that have aged for 18 months in cask will also be bottled. Barrels are blended into tanks before bottling so that all the wine is homogenous, reducing eventual bottle variation. And all the equipment has to be clean and sterile, whether corks or screwcaps are used as the closure. Those wines that are ageing in barrel also need attention, such as periodic racking from one cask to another in order to separate the clear wine from the deposit of lees in the container, both clarifying and aerating at the same time. Great Chardonnays, such as fine white Burgundy, may also be subject to lees stirring in the cask to increase flavour. In Champagne, the *assemblage* of the still wines is followed by the second fermentation in bottle, obtained by adding a mixture of wine, sugar and selected yeast culture to give the bubble in the final result.

For the consumer, perhaps the spring activity that provides the most interest is the first tasting of the new wine in Bordeaux. This is the *futures*, or *primeurs*, market and applies to the great and the good among the châteaux. The producers allow the wine trade and wine commentators to taste samples from cask of the most recent vintage, prior to the first offers of these wines in May, or even June. A great deal of money rides on these judgements and a certain tension is in the air. Buyers have to put down their money two years before they will receive the wine, so care should be taken when choosing a supplier. The fine wine market is now totally international, whether it is for these top young wines, or for more mature, ready-to-drink vintages that can be acquired at auction.

A bird's eye view of Krug Clos du Mesnil in springtime

MENUS
by Laura Greenfield

Lemon Ricotta Stuffed Courgette Flowers,
Mizuna & Tarragon Dressing

Guinea Fowl Pot-Au-Feu
with Spring Vegetables & Tarragon Dumplings

Trio of Chocolate

Smoked Chicken Waldorf Salad

Seared Tuna with Broad Bean,
Avocado & Watermelon Salad

Champagne & Alphonso Mango Jelly
with Mango Cream

SPRING WINES

by Serena Sutcliffe MW

STARTERS

With spring in the air and notoriously difficult-to-match asparagus on the menu, the answer is Sotheby's Champagne! Lemon ricotta courgette flowers would like it too, but the smoked chicken waldorf salad would be more at home with a crisp-as-celery Savoie white.

MAINS

The roast Mediterranean vegetables and Parmesan polenta lend themselves to a vivid Mediterranean red from Sicily, or an Italian grape variety, such as Sangiovese, from Argentina. The guinea fowl pot-au-feu cries out for a red Burgundy from the Côte de Beaune, maybe a Savigny or a Volnay, while I would go for a classic Claret with the veal t-bone – a good petit château, or one of Bordeaux's many excellent *crus bourgeois*. Seared tuna is a solid fish – I would love a red Carmenère from Chile with this, or an Umbrian Sagrantino di Montefalco.

DESSERTS

Eton mess would be even more delicious with a glass of cold Barsac, try the trio of chocolate with a vin santo from Chianti or a Tawny Port and throw caution to the winds with a splash of pink Champagne to accompany the Champagne and Mango Jelly.

Summer

David Hockney describes how he sought to capture on canvas the sudden splash of water created as a diver breaks the surface of a swimming pool: '…it takes me two weeks to paint this event that lasts two seconds. Everyone knows a splash can't be frozen in time, so when you see it like that in a painting it's even more striking than in a photograph'. This painting, made in 1966, sold for £2,920,000 ($5,407,407) in London in 2006 and is the second in a series of three, the largest of which is in the collection of Tate Modern

The unusual colour of this soup is uplifted by the red salsa, white cream and green avocado

Cuban Blackbean Soup with Cumin Crackers, Sour Cream & Salsa

Serves 4 • Preparation time: 1 hour and 8 hours or overnight for soaking beans • Cooking time: 40 minutes
• Pre-heat oven to 180 °C/ 350 °F/ gas-mark 4

Soup

175 g/ 6 oz/ 1 cup black turtle beans, soaked for 8 hours or overnight

200 g/ 7 oz red onion, peeled and finely sliced

2 garlic cloves, peeled and sliced

1½ tsp ground cumin

14 g/ ½ oz fresh ginger, peeled and roughly chopped

3 heaped dessert spoons roughly chopped coriander

1 litre/ 1¾ pints/ 4½ cups chicken stock (page 154)

Avocado Salsa

½ ripe avocado

¼ red onion, peeled and finely sliced

3 cherry tomatoes, quartered with seeds removed and sliced into strips

1 dessert spoon lime juice

To Serve

4 tsp sour cream

Coriander sprigs

Cumin crackers (page 155)

Prepare the chicken stock (page 154) and the cumin crackers beforehand (page 155). Begin the soup by draining and rinsing the soaked black beans. Pour some olive oil into a large saucepan and add the onions, cook for 5 minutes until softened but not browned, then add the garlic, cumin, ginger and coriander and stir for a couple of minutes. Add the black beans and stir in the chicken stock. Bring to boiling point and skim any scum from the surface. Simmer for 40 minutes until the beans are soft before liquidizing to a smooth consistency. Season to taste and thin down with more stock if necessary.

For the salsa, peel and roughly chop the avocado, mix with the onion, tomatoes and lime juice. Lightly season.

Ladle the soup into bowls with the salsa and the sour cream on top. Decorate with coriander and serve with cumin crackers.

Tabbouleh is a light Middle Eastern salad, with the addition of lamb and fritters, it becomes more substantial

Salad of Lamb, Apricot Tabbouleh, Aubergine Fritters & Lemon Aioli

Serves 4 • Preparation time: 1 hour • Cooking time: 10 minutes • Pre-heat oven 220 °C/ 450 °F/ gas-mark 7
• Pre-heat oil to 190 °C/ 375 °F

2 lamb rumps, 200 g/ 7 oz each

Tabbouleh

50 g/ 2 oz/ ¹/₃ cup cracked wheat

1 ripe tomato, quartered, deseeded and diced

3 heaped dessert spoons roughly chopped flat leaf parsley

3 heaped dessert spoons roughly chopped mint

6 dried apricots, finely diced

1 spring onion, finely sliced

1 dessert spoon lemon juice

2 dessert spoons olive oil

Aubergine Fritters

1 small aubergine, cut into 5 mm. (¹/₄ in.) slices

Beer batter (page 154)

300 ml/ ¹/₂ pint vegetable oil for frying

To Serve

Lemon aioli (page 150)

While soaking the cracked wheat in cold water for 20 minutes, prepare the lemon aioli (page 150) and beer batter (page 154). Drain the wheat and squeeze dry. Mix all the tabbouleh ingredients together, season to taste and set aside.

Season the lamb rumps then brown both sides in a hot frying pan. Transfer to the oven and cook for a further 7 minutes, then remove and leave to rest for 5 minutes.

Coat the slices of aubergine with the batter, then cook in the oil until golden brown, before removing and draining on kitchen paper. Sprinkle with a little salt.

Place a few spoonfuls of tabbouleh on each plate, slice the lamb thinly and rest a few pieces against the tabbouleh. Top with a couple of fritters and serve with lemon aioli.

To ensure a better texture for the squid, slice half a kiwi over it and leave for half an hour, allowing the acidity of the fruit to soften the sinew of the squid without affecting its flavour

SAUTÉED SQUID
WITH ARTICHOKE, ROCKET SALAD & CHILLI JAM

Serves 4 • Preparation time: 40 minutes • Cooking time: 20 minutes

275 g/ 10 oz cleaned squid

Salad

50 g/ 2 oz rocket

Globe artichokes (page 156)

100 ml/ 3¹/₂ fl oz/ ¹/₂ cup lime dressing (page 153)

To Serve

4 tsp chilli jam (page 155)

First, prepare the lime dressing (page 153), chilli jam (page 155) and globe artichokes (page 156). Once these are all ready, slice open the squid lengthways and score the inside surface lightly in a criss-cross pattern without cutting all the way through. Cut into 5 cm. (2 in.) pieces. Preheat a pan and add a little vegetable oil, season the squid and place each piece scored side down first. They will start to curl when cooked. Toss them around the pan for another minute then take off the heat.

Toss the rocket and artichokes with a little of the lime dressing, divide between plates with the squid and a teaspoon of chilli jam on top of each and drizzle with the remaining lime dressing.

Frank R. Paul is universally recognised as the father of all modern science fiction artwork. This futuristic original cover for Science Wonder Quarterly, published in the Winter 1930 issue, was from the Sam Moskowitz Collection of Science Fiction and sold for $76,750 (£48,352) in New York in June 1999

Appetite for Knowledge

Becoming one of the world's great bestsellers, Isabella Beeton's *Book of Household Management* was first printed as a complete book in 1861. The popularity of the book means that first editions – such as that shown left which sold for £1,207 ($1,988) in London in 1999 – are rare. An interesting insight into the life of Isabella Beeton was afforded when a group of letters written by her to her then fiancé appeared at auction in 1997

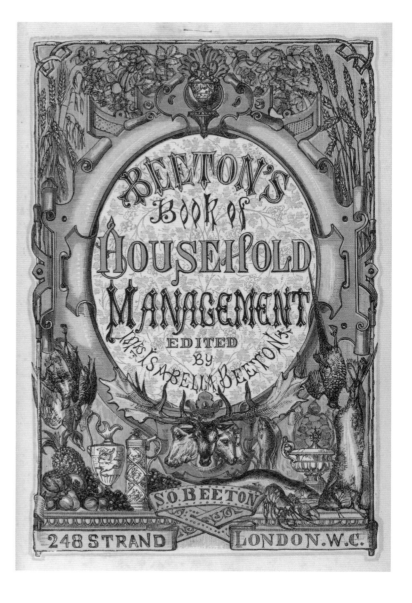

William Sitwell, editor of Waitrose Food Illustrated magazine, and Kathryn Hughes, historian and author of The Short Life and Long Times of Mrs Beeton, analyse the history and purpose of food writing and cookery books with Paul Quarrie, a keen cook and senior director of the Book department at Sotheby's London

Paul Quarrie: I am curious to know if you both think that food writing seems to be split into writing about eating food and recipe or cookery books?

Kathryn Hughes: I think that food writing has fulfiled many different roles at different times, so it's impossible to come up with a single answer to embrace everything. It records what already exists; it advocates what could or should happen.

William Sitwell: To me, the most important aspect is the quality of the writing and the ability to communicate. A food writer has to be a writer first and foremost. The various aspects of food writing are also different – for example, recipe writing is an art in itself and someone like Nigella Lawson engages the reader and explains what is taking place.

PQ: Food appears in the earliest written texts, from Homer and the Bible onwards – but often is present as a precise description of food, due to the important symbolism and significance of eating a meal. Food writing draws upon that communal idea of sharing food, as recorded in the account of the Last Supper and by Classical writers such as Virgil or Athenaeus, and continues in the Renaissance and in novels such as *Tom Jones* and *A Christmas Carol*. It is something that Elizabeth David did incredibly well.

WS: She was primarily a great communicator, in the same way that earlier authors such as Eliza Acton and Hannah Glasse in the 18th century were. Those books are completely different to some of the ghostwritten, celebrity cookery books that one sees currently – great recipe writers engage in both the subject and the process of writing. In the case of earlier cookery writers, it was often the first time that the recipes had been recorded and made available to people who were not servants.

PQ: Absolutely, there was a tradition in aristocratic houses of writing down menus and methods for things that had worked well over the years. I am sure that many of the chatelaines of those great country houses had a book for giving instructions and managing the house. There are a lot of manuscript cookbooks in circulation, particularly from the 18th and 19th century – we have them appearing in auctions all the time, in English, French, German and Norwegian.

WS: The great thing about those books is their practical authenticity. They were integral to running the house.

KH: That aristocratic tradition derives from the need to communicate recipes within a large household. I have seen recipes from the 18th century, which are precisely dated with when the meal was eaten, so any aspect of a great dinner can be recreated. What makes someone like Hannah Glasse interesting is that she was writing for the middle classes and was one of the first writers to codify what was normally passed from mother to daughter. In fact, she was quite scathing about the aristocracy, with their French chefs and 'French trickery'. It was so proudly bourgeois – and she needed to make money from it.

WS: It was the beginning of a recognition that a market for these books actually existed.

KH: Absolutely, and all of these books open with the protestation that they are writing to instruct and have done so at the prompting of friends, but really they are commercial ventures.

PQ: I imagine though, given how publishing worked then, that even those books published in large editions would not necessarily have meant a huge amount of money going to the author.

KH: Elizabeth Raffald, who wrote slightly later than Hannah Glasse, was completely immersed in this new culture of publishing and printing that exploded in the 18th century and, in order to guarantee that the recipes were hers – and to avoid anyone else stealing them – she signed each page of her books.

WS: Borrowing and adapting recipes is part of cookery writing though. I think plagiarism is the wrong word, there is no definitive recipe for scrambled eggs for instance. You get it from one book, then add chives, cream, or salmon. Perhaps it is slightly different with restaurants but fundamentally, people understand that you are always going to use different sources for inspiration.

PQ: In some respects that is a modern practice and the codification of certain recipes as the definitive version is quite recent.

WS: It is important to recognise originality, so something like fusion cooking is a really inventive use of different recipes. People always try to experiment with dishes, so I suppose a move to return to the perceived original or traditional format for a dish is a trend like any other.

PQ: In a sense, the process of recording in cookery books inhibits some inventiveness, because of offering a definitive version, and it means that people are less likely to experiment or create dishes from memory.

KH: What's interesting is that people still retain the fantasy of an original somewhere. My research on Mrs Beeton showed that she was as open as anyone to adapting recipes, but it was reported in the press that 'Mrs Beeton was a plagiarist'.

WS: That is also dependent on who is perceived as the authority at the time, or who is most marketable, whose version of a recipe had the greatest currency. So Mrs Beeton was consulted by every Victorian and Edwardian household.

KH: That is certainly how she was perceived in the popular imagination. As with all great texts, in fact there is no real way of

knowing how the book was actually used, and this is even more the case for an author such as Mrs Beeton. It is far less likely that the amendments and alterations to recipes that took place in the kitchen would have been recorded. I suppose one of the reasons that Mrs Beeton is so interesting is that her story coincides with an amazing growth of print culture, with the ability to print more cheaply making information accessible to a vast audience. Her books replaced some of the oral traditions that had existed before the population became more mobile. So instead of consulting their mothers about the traditional ways of managing a household, young women referred to Mrs Beeton.

WS: Rose Prince is another important cookery writer, whose book *New English Kitchen* has similar elements of teaching a new way to shop, eat, and manage food.

KH: When I read Rose Prince I immediately think of her as similar to Mrs Beeton at her best, full of useful advice and ideas.

WS: I do think that people still read recipe books as recreation, and then take the recipe as inspiration and adapt it to the ingredients that they have in the house. Having said that, the proliferation of illustrated cookery books and television shows makes one feel that one should try and emulate the pictures exactly.

PQ: I have some books dating from the 1960s, with grand visions of what was served in huge silver dishes in restaurants, which was distinctly off-putting. Similarly books produced around the Second World War, which had such dreadful, grainy photographs that would have inspired anyone to make the recipes. They were so different from today's cookery books, and reflected different times and a different attitude to food: more eat to live than live to eat.

KH: I can imagine the kind of extraordinary burst of excitement when Elizabeth David's books came out. I think her first, *A Book of Mediterranean Cookery*, has a tremendous sense of the possibilities of food and the pleasure of eating.

PQ: I am an enormous admirer of her – one that of the few places she could find olive oil was in chemists, where it was sold in tiny bottles as a treatment for earache. I have her copy of Athenaeus' *Deipnosophistae [Wise Men at Dinner]*, which I absolutely cherish. The vigour in her writing is immense and her ability to conjure up visions and tastes of the Mediterranean is extraordinary.

WS: Her idea that you can write interestingly about an omelette was such a revelation, and when you read her descriptions of how to make an omelette, you realise that there's an amazing history even with something so straight forward, and it legitimised the fact that simplicity could be interesting.

KH: I love how she invests the ordinary with such a sense of art and wonder, which makes even an everyday dish becomes a whole experience.

WS: That passion for food has become much more mainstream. Elizabeth David sparked an interest in food and sang the praises of British food as well, naming specific places to visit to obtain ingredients. I think, to some extent, she looked for some of that peasant heritage, which comes across in so much French and Italian cookery, which we have more or less lost.

KH: She developed the idea that because we had an Industrial Revolution first, we lost those pockets of peasant food, and then along came Mrs Beeton and codified recipes to reflect her urban middle-class life. Although that assessment is a little unfair as it suggests that Mrs Beeton, who was only 21 at the time she started writing, single-handedly stamped out the tradition of peasant cookery in Britain. The industrial revolution had achieved that and Mrs Beeton's book happened to be written at the same time.

PQ: Britain's history of plain fare – roast beef and so on – and great periods of rural poverty meant that many in the countryside ate incredibly badly.

WS: I was travelling in Romania recently and saw a huge number of small holdings, which is essentially the peasant lifestyle, with people subsisting from a patch of land and one or two livestock. So the food is entirely regional, local and seasonal – and totally subsistence. That means that during certain seasons there is really very little food available and not much variety, which does make me appreciate supermarkets.

KH: I think that one of the dominant fantasies at the moment is seasonality. To eat in this manner rigorously though, February would not be fun.

PQ: Trends such as that however prove how much interest there is in food and the provenance of food at the moment. Do all these cookery books make for better cooking?

WS: Well, more cookery books are sold now than ever before, but it is hard to know exactly how they are used and even the popularity of food programmes belies the fact that most people watch them for entertainment rather than instruction. While there may be a gulf that still exists, we now have an amazing array of ingredients from around the world, with wonderful organic food, and a huge variety of books and so on to chose from.

PQ: I suppose that the reality of being guided through the world of food and ingredients by someone like Elizabeth David – or indeed Mrs Beeton – is an extraordinary journey that will continue to be undertaken.

A Book of Mediterranean Food was the first of Elizabeth David's hugely influential series of cookery books. The striking cover of the first edition from 1950 wonderfully conveys the completely fresh approach to food that was advocated within

An interesting insight into the life of Isabella Beeton (opposite) was afforded when a group of letters written by her to her then fiancé appeared at auction in 1997 when they sold for £8,625 ($13,945)

Tomatoes are fantastic roasted. They add a wonderful flavour and colour to a dish

Pesto Risotto Cakes with Roast Cherry Tomatoes & Parmesan

Serves 4 • Preparation time: 1 hour • Cooking time: 40 minutes • Cooling time: 2 hours • Pre-heat oven to 200 °C/ 400 °F/ gas-mark 6

Risotto Cakes

50 g/ 2 oz unsalted butter

100 g/ 4 oz/ 1 cup grated Parmesan

Double amount of risotto (page 157)

275 g/ 10 oz basil pesto (page 154)

Polenta for coating

Roast Tomatoes

350 g/ 12 oz cherry tomatoes on the vine

To Serve

75 g/ 3 oz rocket

50 g/ 2 oz Parmesan shavings

First prepare the basil pesto (page 154) and cook the risotto (page 157). Then stir the butter and grated Parmesan into the risotto and season to taste. Spoon the mixture onto a flat tray and cool for 2 hours.

Place the tomatoes on a baking tray, season and drizzle with olive oil, place in the oven for 8–10 minutes until they are soft but retain their shape.

When cool, mix the risotto with the basil pesto, shape into 8 cakes and coat with the polenta. Heat some vegetable oil in a large frying pan and cook the cakes until golden brown on both sides, being careful not to overcrowd the pan, then transfer to an oven tray and cook for 4 minutes.

Arrange the rocket and roast tomatoes on a plate, put two cakes to the side and sprinkle over the Parmesan shavings.

It-alia, constructed in mirror crystal and lead on wood, is part of a series of sculptures made by the Arte Povera artist, Luciano Fabro, in varying materials and forms using the shape of Italy as inspiration. It sold for £113,500 ($160,310) at the Contemporary Art sale in London in February 2002

Barbary Duck Breast with Soba Noodles, Bok Choy & Tataki Dressing

Serves 4 • Preparation time 1½ hours • Cooking time 10 minutes • Pre-heat the oven to 220 °C/ 475 °F/ gas-mark 7 • Pre-heat the oil to 160 °C/ 325 °F

Eastern spices are a mainstay of contemporary British cuisine. The exotic aromas of the ginger and soy in the Tataki sauce fuse delicately with the duck

2 shallots, peeled and finely sliced lengthways

250 ml/ ¹/₂ pint/ 1¹/₈ cups vegetable oil for frying

2 large red chillies, deseeded and finely sliced

100 g/ 4 oz sliced shiitake mushrooms

4 dessert spoons sesame oil

4 duck breasts, 225 g/ 8 oz each

275 g/ 10 oz soba (buckwheat) noodles, cooked and cooled

2 heads bok choy, washed, quartered and blanched

4 spring onions, finely sliced at an angle

150 ml/ ¹/₄ pint/ 1¹/₈ cups Tataki sauce (page 152)

Coriander sprigs

While the oil is heating, make the Tataki sauce (page 152). Then, drop the shallots into the hot oil, stirring occasionally for about 3–5 minutes until golden brown and drain onto kitchen paper. In the same oil, cook the chillies until dark red and set aside. Sauté the shiitake mushrooms in sesame oil over a moderate heat until golden brown. Lightly season and set aside.

Trim any excess fat from the duck and score the remaining fat in a criss-cross pattern, being careful not to cut into the flesh. Season the duck breasts well and place the skin side down in a hot frying pan over a moderate flame and brown on both sides. Put into the oven for 6–8 minutes and then leave to stand for 5 minutes.

Mix the noodles, bok choy, sautéed mushrooms, spring onions and the Tataki sauce and divide between plates. Slice the duck and place beside the noodles, then pour over a little more sauce, sprinkle the fried shallots and chillies on top and garnish with coriander.

The currants add an interesting sweetness to this dish and combine well with the salsa verde and herb crust

ROAST HAKE WITH HERB CRUST, BRAISED FENNEL & SALSA VERDE

Serves 4 • Preparation time: 30 minutes • Cooking time: 1 hour • Pre-heat oven to 200 °C/ 400 °F/ gas-mark 6

4 hake steaks, 200 g/ 7 oz each

Herb Crust

1 heaped dessert spoon finely chopped dill

1 heaped dessert spoon finely chopped chervil

1 heaped dessert spoon finely chopped chives

1 heaped dessert spoon finely chopped tarragon

1 heaped dessert spoon finely chopped flat leaf parsley

25 g/ 1 oz/ ½ cup fresh breadcrumbs

1 heaped dessert spoon chopped currants (optional)

Braised Fennel

2 fennel bulbs

300 ml/ ½ pint/ 1¼ cups chicken stock (page 154)

Splash white wine

10 strands saffron

50 g/ 2 oz butter

To Serve

Salsa verde (page 151)

Sprigs of chervil

Prepare the salsa verde (page 151) and chicken stock (page 154). Cut the fennel bulbs into quarters and place in an ovenproof dish, pour over the stock and wine, add the saffron strands, half of the butter and lightly season. Cover with foil and place in the oven for 50 minutes until the fennel is soft. Remove the fennel from the dish and reduce the juice by half before setting aside.

For the crust, mix the herbs with the breadcrumbs, season and add the currants if you wish. Heat a large ovenproof frying pan, add some vegetable oil, season the hake steaks and brown on both sides. Roast in the oven for 6 minutes, then remove and sprinkle the herb crumbs on each steak and place the fennel pieces flat in the pan. Return to the oven for a further 5 minutes. Warm the fennel juice and whisk in the remaining butter.

Place the fish in the centre of each plate with two pieces of fennel on either side. Pour a little of the fennel juice around and spoon over the salsa verde. Garnish with sprigs of chervil.

THE LOBSTER CLUB

Makes 4 sandwiches • Preparation time: 1 hour

After ten years this club sandwich remains one of the Cafe's most popular dishes

Lobster

2 cooked lobsters weighing approximately
600 g/ 1 lb 5 oz each

200 ml/ 7 fl oz/ 1 cup lemon aioli (page 150)

12 splashes Tabasco

Juice of ¹/₂ lemon

To Serve

12 slices brioche

¹/₂ iceberg lettuce, thinly sliced

4 ripe tomatoes, sliced and grilled until soft

8 rashers of bacon, cooked and roughly chopped

Begin by preparing the lemon aioli (page 150). To extract the lobster meat from the shell, first remove the claws then, using a lobster cracker or the blunt end of a heavy knife, crack the shells open and take out the meat. Next remove the head and discard, take off the remaining tail section and cut along the softer shell of the underside. The meat should come out in one piece, then slice in half lengthways and discard the dark vein running through the middle. Roughly chop all the lobster meat, bind with the aioli, Tabasco and lemon juice and season to taste.

Lightly toast the brioche slices, leaving four aside for the top slice. Divide the lettuce between the remaining eight slices, followed by the tomatoes, lobster mix and a generous sprinkling of bacon. Lift one layer on top of another to make a double-decker, followed by the top slice of brioche, and secure with a cocktail stick in each corner. Cut each sandwich into quarters and serve with a glass of champagne.

One of many sensational collaborations between the designer Elsa Schiaparelli's and the Surrealist artist Salvador Dalí, was this 'lobster dress' worn by the Duchess of Windsor, photographed here by Sir Cecil Beaton. The renowned photographer sold his studio archive to Sotheby's in 1977

The Last Supper

Andy Warhol was commissioned
to create a series of works based
on Leonardo da Vinci's Last
Supper. They were exhibited
across the street from the
original work in Milan. His
treatments reveal a fascination
with the relationship between
high and low art. This example,
which dates from 1986, sold
at Sotheby's New York in 2003
for $1,800,000 (£1,081,276)

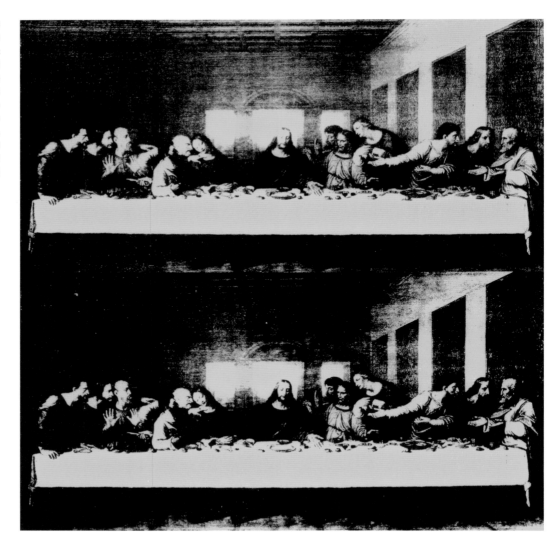

Tim Marlow, broadcaster and exhibitions director at the White Cube Gallery, and Carolin Young, art and food historian, analyse the enduring appeal and significance of the Last Supper with Gregory Rubinstein, head of the Old Master Drawings department at Sotheby's in London

Gregory Rubinstein: It is fascinating that the Last Supper comes up repeatedly in western art history, did the scene always have a singular significance or was it part of the wider story of Christ?

Carolin Young: The biblical story in the Passion of Christ is the tale of Christ gathering his disciples around him for the last time and it is the moment when he declares that he will be betrayed three times, and Judas is revealed as the one who will betray him by dipping his hands in the wine bowl. It is also the introduction of the Eucharist – the blessing of the bread and wine.

GR: I believe that the earliest depiction of the subject is a mosaic in Ravenna – from around the 6th century.

CY: Indeed, that is the earliest I have found. It is in the San Apollinare Nuovo in Ravenna and the date to me is very revealing as it relates to how we view the Last Supper. There appear to be no versions before the 6th century, even though it is a central event in the Christian tradition.

Tim Marlow: Although it is probably the first version of the subject, it does not actually set the tone for subsequent depictions, I think, because Christ is on the left-hand side and, whereas in most other versions, he takes the central position. There are also fish in this specific mosaic, which has strong Christian symbolism but is not an accurate depiction of what they might have eaten at that particular supper.

CY: The food that is depicted in most treatments of the Last Supper – particularly those Renaissance versions that have become the staple image – varies radically according to who the image was intended for. Some versions feature more rustic food, others seafood or roast meats.

TM: I suppose bread was the only staple – which is Eucharistic as well as part of any diet.

GR: …and the wine presumably.

CY: Strangely even those elements are not constant, the bread is often not the unleavened kind used in church ceremonies, and some paintings such as a series in Alto Adige and parts of the Veneto, which would have been seen mainly by peasants, become almost a celebration of the abundance of food. These depictions show red or white wine according to which is made in the local town, crayfish, and an immense variety of breads. The northern-most example, close to Austria, shows pretzels on the table. Going back to the Ravenna mosaic, it does contain some elements that are more accurate, for instance it is probable they would have been reclining because apparently, wherever you were in the Roman Empire, this was considered the sign of being a free man.

TM: Christ is also wearing the purple robe of the Roman Emperor in that image.

GR: Is it right to assume that the depiction of the Last Supper as a subject in its own right as Da Vinci treated it rather than as part of the medieval Passion cycle, began during the Renaissance?

CY: It really was a Renaissance development. The 15th-century tradition of painting the Last Supper on its own in the Refectory is significant in that the image is of dining but would also become part of the experience of the meal for the monks who would be eating in the room. While, of course, a whole line of painters play with that image, Da Vinci's version in Milan is really the apogée of that phenomenon and becomes its defining version.

GR: The composition of the Da Vinci Last Supper, with that long table, was, in some ways, dictated by being painted for a refectory, but I suppose there are relatively few other ways you can portray the subject. It is much harder to make it a round table and show everyone clearly without creating a very confused space. I think this has definitely conditioned a lot of the versions – the Da Vinci version became the definitive prototype of the image.

Selling in London in 2001 for £179,500 ($252,532), Sir Peter Paul Rubens' pen and ink drawing of the Last Supper (above) was probably designed to be turned into an etching for a book on religious ceremonies and observances

Damien Hirst created a myriad of artworks for the renowned Pharmacy restaurant in London, of which he was the co-owner. This example, shown opposite, sold as part of a series of 13 works entitled Last Supper in London for £45,600 ($82,014)

TM: It is interesting that Tintoretto seems to deliberately skew Da Vinci's composition and paints the protagonists from all sorts of different angles. Sometimes frontal but often diagonal, I suppose the subject becomes a vehicle for artists to show their grasp of space and perspective in relation to the drama of the scene. Giotto, long before Da Vinci, painted the Last Supper using perspective and with the disciples both facing us and with their backs to us and with Christ at the head of the table on the left hand side.

GR: Considering that the Da Vinci version has become an iconic image, is painting it in a different form a challenge to the received notion of the subject?

CY: I think part of that is to do with the sense of appropriateness for what a sacred picture should be. Tintoretto shows details of the wine flasks in his works, while Veronese, famously criticised by the Inquisition for having too many Germans and dwarves and even forks in his version of the subject, was ultimately compelled to rename it *The Feast in the House of Levi*.

TM: Do you think Veronese was trying to be provocative when the Inquisition said he had made a mockery of the Last Supper?

CY: Well his defence to the Inquisition about the freedom of an artist to express himself is very famous and makes one think he must have wanted to shock to some extent. To my mind though, and from everything I have read, he was genuinely surprised by the official reaction and, of course, Venice did have a more independent relationship with the church. I think it didn't occur to him to think of it as anything other than a spectacular celebratory feast. This debate about religious art has gone on for centuries in all religions: are you celebrating God by making a splendid feast or by abstaining from the pleasures of life?

GR: It bears an interesting comparison with some contemporary versions of the subject, which challenge not only Da Vinci's famous composition but also religious beliefs and ideas. I wonder how much of that is driven by a desire to shock?

TM: Well, I don't think a work like Sam Taylor-Wood's *Wrecked*, which had a woman in the position of Christ, was simply intended to shock. When it was displayed in 1996 at the Sensation exhibition at the Royal Academy, she said it was a response to the freedom and hedonism of the time and that she wanted to create a kind of crazy dinner party. Very consciously in her case, in choosing the Last Supper, one of the most iconic dinners ever painted in art history, and, because she's a female artist and she chose a woman in the Christ-like pose in the centre, people thought it was a feminist statement. Again though I don't believe it is that explicit, in that image the woman is ignored by everyone else, and seems to be in a different, liberated state, and and there's that moment of sublime freedom or intoxication. In a way it's profound and mundane. Interestingly though the way Sam Taylor-Wood staged it was as much a homage to the likes of Caravaggio and Derek Jarman as it was to Da Vinci. I think the composition of the Last Supper was simply a springboard to depict something contemporary and I don't think it has religious overtones in any way whatsoever.

GR: How much can a work like Chris Ofili's *Upper Room*, which is now in Tate Britain, be compared to Da Vinci's *Last Supper*?

TM: I think it is a starting point again. Each of the paintings for *Upper Room* are named after a colour, not a disciple, and there is a Christ-like figure at the centre. It could relate back to Veronese making a mockery of the Last Supper, but actually the use of monkeys in a post-Darwinian world is making a point about origins – monkeys are not sinful or playful but are our ancestors. On another level it deals with so called 'primitive art'.

There is another connection with Da Vinci, who in the refectory in Milan did not created a naturalistic depiction but manipulated perspective so that the monks would feel part of this extraordinary *trompe l'oeil*. This is something Ofili does very powerfully in the *Upper Room* paintings, placing the viewer right in the middle of this visual feast.

GR: Another contemporary depiction, which appeared in the Pharmacy sale held at Sotheby's a few years ago, was Damien Hirst's set of 13 medicine packets entitled *Last Supper* – did he also execute a version with ping-pong balls?

TM: No, it's an unrealised work as yet. My understanding of it is 13 balls held up by jets of blood. Hirst moved away from his religious upbringing but his art continues to reverberate with Catholic and Christian iconographic references, although many of those references are more universal than specifically cultural. It is said that Warhol's depiction of Da Vinci's *Last Supper* relate to his Polish Catholic background – his family went regularly to the church in Pittsburgh and his mother remained a practising Catholic throughout her life. He clearly had some relationship with religion, but I think in his case he treated Da Vinci's work in the same way that he treated his self-portraits or images of celebrities. It becomes a commodity, which is also what Damien Hirst is looking at when he made his version of the Last Supper using pill packets. Each of the pills were replaced by mundane foods, which not only relates to the idea of The Last Supper but also to the concept of it becoming a kind of brand. The idea of this image becoming so familiar that its meaning is almost lost because of mass production.

GR: I wondered if Da Vinci's work has become so reproduced that it has actually lost religious significance?

TM: Like any image, the more it's reproduced the more it loses its power, but what's fascinating about the *Last Supper* is that it began to fade within Da Vinci's lifetime, so we have never seen the whole image. It takes on this almost holographic presence, flickering in and out of our imagination.

GR: I suppose, of all the scenes of the Passion, by depicting a meal, the Last Supper is closest, at least superficially, to scenes of modern life. In a way it is natural that this image should be picked up on by contemporary artists.

CY: It is also important to understand why, during the Renaissance, the Last Supper had an additional significance. The Humanists and Neo-Platonists recognised the significance of the scene as a meal, a symposium. That idea of individuals getting together and remaining individuals within a group, which is very much what modern culture is based upon.

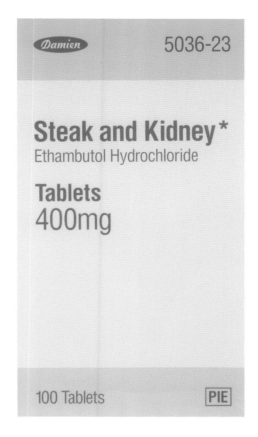

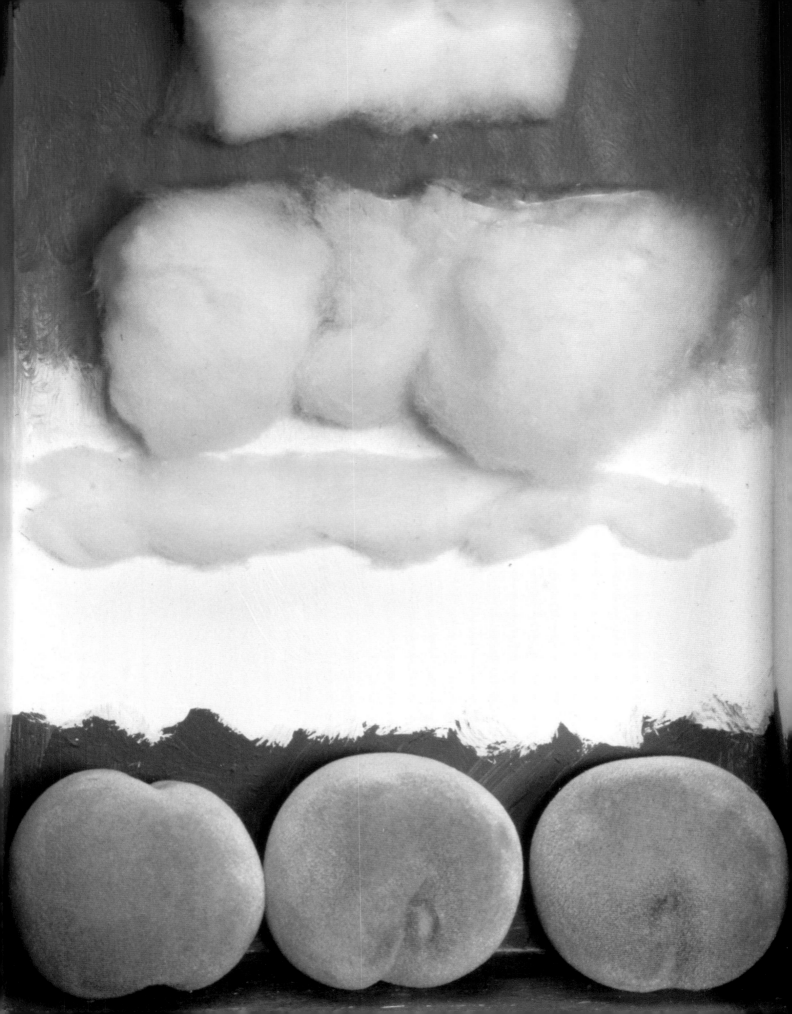

The inspiration for this sorbet comes from Harry's Bar in Venice – the result epitomises the taste of summer

Bellini Sorbet with White Peach & Mint Syrup

Serves 4 • Makes 1 litre/ 1³/₄ pints • Preparation time: 45 minutes • Freezing time: 2 hours

250 ml/ 9 fl oz/ 1 cup water

150 g/ 5 oz/ 1¹/₈ cups caster sugar

125 ml/ 4¹/₂ fl oz/ ¹/₃ cup liquid glucose

10 blanched mint leaves, finely chopped

7 ripe white peaches (5 for the juice and 2 for serving)

200 ml/ 7 fl oz/ 1 cup Prosecco

50 ml/ 2 fl oz/ ¹/₄ cup lemon juice

Put the water and sugar in a saucepan and stir until the sugar dissolves before boiling the mixture for 5 minutes. Add the liquid glucose and then let it cool completely, setting aside 3 dessert spoons to which the mint leaves should be added, before storing the syrup in the fridge until serving.

Quarter 5 of the peaches, remove the stones and juice them to measure out 400 ml/ 14 fl oz/ 1³/₄ cups. Mix the sugar syrup with the peach juice, Prosecco and lemon juice, strain and place in an ice-cream machine, filling up to half way only. Churn until firm enough to scoop, then scrape out into a plastic container, cover and place in the freezer for 2 hours.

Slice the remaining peaches into discs, fan around the plates, place a scoop of Bellini sorbet in the middle and drizzle with mint syrup.

Man Ray's Pêchage, a detail of which is shown here, was created with plastic peaches, cotton wool and oil, all enclosed in a wooden box, and sold in London in 1995 for £47,700 ($75,843). Ten years later, Sotheby's sold a similar work from the same series, which achieved an astonishing £105,600 ($195,918)

The key to a good strudel is in the lightness of the pastry, from there, the filling can be adapted according to which fruits are in season

BLACKBERRY & APPLE STRUDEL

Serves 4–6 • Preparation time: 45 minutes • Cooking time: 20–25 minutes • Pre-heat oven to 200 °C/ 400 °F/ gas-mark 6

Strudel

150 g/ 5 oz/ 1¹/₃ cup plain flour

1 dessert spoon vegetable oil

¹/₂ beaten egg

75 ml/ 2¹/₂ fl oz/ ³/₄ cup tepid water

50 g/ 2 oz melted butter

2 dessert spoons breadcrumbs

Filling

400 g/ 1 lb Bramley apples, peeled, cored and quartered

150 g/ 5 oz blackberries

1 level tsp cinnamon

50 g/ 2 oz/ ¹/₃ cup sultanas

50 g/ 2 oz/ ¹/₂ cup walnut pieces

125 g/ 4¹/₂ oz/ ¹/₂ cup caster sugar

To Serve

Icing sugar and double cream to taste

Place the flour in a mixing bowl, make a well in the centre and add the vegetable oil, egg and water to make a soft dough. Knead for 2 minutes on a floured surface until the dough is smooth and not sticky. Lightly oil a piece of cling film, wrap up the dough and leave out until needed.

For the filling, cut the apples into thin slices and place in a bowl with the blackberries, cinnamon, sultanas, walnuts and caster sugar. Mix well and set aside.

Flour a worktop and roll the pastry to a 3 mm. (¹/₈ in.) thickness, then liberally flour a tea towel and lift the dough onto it. Carefully pull the pastry on all sides until it is thin, almost transparent. It should measure 30 by 50 cm. (12 by 20 in.). Gently brush with half of the melted butter, sprinkle over the breadcrumbs and scatter the apple mix evenly over the surface. Pull the thicker pieces of excess pastry off the edges, fold in the sides and using the tea towel roll up into a strudel. Lift the strudel onto a large baking tray lined with baking parchment, making sure that the join of the pastry is on the underside, brush with remaining butter and dust generously with icing sugar. Bake for 20–25 minutes until the pastry is golden brown and leave to cool before serving. Cut into thick slices and serve with cream.

Rocky road is great fun to prepare and delicious with strawberries, especially in the heat of summer

Strawberries & Rocky Road

Serves 4 • Preparation time: 15 minutes • Setting time: 2 hours

450 g/ 1 lb strawberries

Rocky Road

175 g/ 6 oz plain chocolate

50 g/.2 oz/ ⅓ cup glacé cherries

50 g/ 2 oz/ ⅓ cup whole roasted almonds

100 g/ 4 oz/ 1 cup marshmallows

To Serve

75 ml/ 3 fl oz double cream

Icing sugar for dusting

Melt the chocolate in a bowl and add the cherries, almonds and marshmallows and mix until they are all coated in chocolate. Line a baking tray with grease-proof paper and spread the mixture evenly on it, set in the fridge for 2 hours.

Cut the rocky road into chunks and place in a bowl with the washed and hulled strawberries. Serve with cream and dust with icing sugar.

A Still Life of Wild Strawberries and a Carnation in a Ming Bowl, was painted in oil on copper by the 17th-century Netherlandish artist Jacob van Huldonck. It sold for £520,500 ($754,020) at the Old Master Paintings sale in London in December 2000

WINE THROUGH THE SEASONS

SUMMER

by Serena Sutcliffe MW

Early summer is the epoch for the flowering of the vine, an exciting moment that can vary enormously according to the amount of warmth experienced after budding. A prolonged bout of good weather can produce early flowering and certain varieties make it to the post before others. The essential ingredient for a healthy harvest, which follows approximately 100 days afterwards, is an even, smooth flowering as this produces bunches of grapes that are equally ripe. Cold, rain and wind can all be harmful at flowering and, in severe cases, ruin a crop and lead to financial difficulties. In areas where there are a mixture of grape varieties, flowering happens at different times for each type, so adverse conditions may only affect one variety, leading later to a wine that will be more, or less, influenced by that grape. This is all part of the fascination of comparing vintages.

We are now well into the growing season and heat, sunlight and rainfall all play their part in determining the ultimate character of the year's wine. Extreme heat can lead to storms – the worst scenario is hail storms, with their concomitant damage to the vineyard and possibly, at late summer stage, influence on the taste of the wine if the hailed grapes are not eliminated. Luckily, hail is almost always very localised, affecting a small plot of vines but not its neighbour. An alert eye must be kept on the health of the vines, watching out for any sign of rot, if conditions are humid, diseases or pests, and spraying if necessary. Increasingly, organic or bio-dynamic methods are used to control these dangers – for instance, encouraging natural predators to ward off certain undesirable insects. Ploughing the vineyards is another summer activity. The grapes change colour between the end of July and the beginning of August in Europe, giving an indication of when they will be ripe and ready to be picked. If the potential crop looks too large, this is the time to reduce yield by knocking off bunches – green harvesting – while leaf thinning now can also increase ripeness.

In the lull before the harvest, many who work at wine properties will try and snatch some holiday before the most frantic time of the year, the culmination of all their efforts. When they return, ready for the fray, they will have to prepare all the picking and cellar equipment, making sure everything is pristine and in perfect order for the reception of the grapes. And then the harvest comes round again – the wonderful, reassuring, cyclic rhythm of the vineyard and of wine.

The celestial Château d'Yquem, the colour of a summer sunset

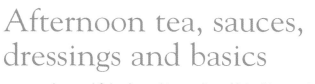

Afternoon tea, sauces, dressings and basics

Leonard Salzer's working replica of John Harrison's first sea-clock, 'H1', sold for $904,000 at the final auction of the New York Time Museum in October 2004. The businessman Seth G. Atwood assembled this fine collection of 3,000 timepieces over a period of more than 30 years.

SAUCES

AIOLI

Makes 200 ml/ 7 fl oz/ 1 cup
Preparation time: 20 minutes

2 egg yolks

1 tsp Dijon mustard

1 garlic clove, crushed to a paste

75 ml/ 3 fl oz/ ⅓ cup vegetable oil

75 ml/ 3 fl oz/ ⅓ cup extra virgin olive oil

3 tsp white wine vinegar

3 tsp water

Put the egg yolks, mustard, garlic and a pinch of salt and pepper in a bowl and whisk the ingredients with an electric mixer until slightly thickened. Slowly pour in both oils, whisking continuously, and then thin down with the vinegar and water. This will keep for a maximum of four days if refrigerated.

Lemon Aioli: substitute the vinegar with 4 teaspoons of lemon juice and the zest of a lemon.

Piquillo Pepper Aioli: after making the aioli, stir in 3 finely processed Piquillo peppers.

CREAMY LEEK SAUCE

Makes 200 ml/ 7 fl oz/ ¾–1 cup
Preparation time: 15 minutes
Cooking time: 10 minutes

25 g/ 1 oz unsalted butter

1 leek, washed, trimmed and finely sliced

1 level dessert spoon plain flour

200 ml/ 7 fl oz/ ¾–1 cup milk reserved from the recipe for smoked haddock soufflé (page 16)

1 heaped dessert spoon chopped chives

Heat the butter, add the leek and sweat until softened. Add the flour, allow to cook for 30 seconds, then gradually pour in the milk, stirring constantly. Allow to boil for 1 minute, then remove from the heat, add the chopped chives and season to taste.

GORGONZOLA SAUCE

Makes 150 ml/ ¼ pint/ ⅔ cup
Cooking time: 5 minutes

75 g/ 3 oz Gorgonzola

75 ml/ 3 fl oz/ ⅓ cup cream

Add pieces of the Gorgonzola to the cream in a saucepan and stir over a gentle heat until melted.

SAUCES

MALTAISE SAUCE

Makes 150 ml/ 5 fl oz/ ²/₃ cup
Preparation time: 30 minutes
Cooking time: 10 minutes

75 ml/ 3 fl oz/ ¹/₃ cup white wine vinegar

1 shallot, finely sliced

3 whole peppercorns

2 egg yolks

Zest of 1 orange and juice of ¹/₄ of an orange
(use blood oranges when in season)

150 g/ 5 oz warmed clarified butter
(page 154)

Salt and cayenne pepper

Prepare the clarified butter (page 154).
Put a small pan of water on to boil.
Place the vinegar, shallot and peppercorns in a stainless steel pan and reduce
until there are 2 dessert spoons of liquid
left, then strain.

Mix the reduced liquid, egg yolks and
orange zest in a bowl and place on top
of the simmering pan of water. Whisk
until the mixture has increased in volume
and lightened in colour. Remove from
the heat and slowly add the clarified
butter, whisking all the time. Season
with salt, a tiny pinch of cayenne pepper
and add the orange juice. Keep in a
warm place – the sauce will keep for an
hour before serving.

PAPRIKA SAUCE

Makes 200 ml/ 7 fl oz/ ³/₄–1 cup
Preparation time: 15 minutes
Cooking time: 15 minutes

25 g/ 1 oz unsalted butter

150 g/ 5 oz onion, finely sliced

1 chopped garlic clove

5 sprigs fresh thyme

1 level dessert spoon paprika

100 ml/ 3¹/₂ tbsp/ ¹/₃ cup dry white wine

200 ml/ 7 fl oz/ ³/₄ cup chicken stock
(page 154)

100 ml/ 3¹/₂ fl oz/ ¹/₃ cup double cream

Melt the butter in a medium-sized
saucepan and gently cook the onions for
10 minutes until soft and golden. Add the
garlic, thyme and paprika and stir for 2
minutes ensuring it does not burn. Pour in
the white wine, turn up the heat and let it
boil down to almost nothing. Add the
stock and reduce by half, then add the
cream, bring to the boil and cook until
slightly thickened. Remove the thyme
sprigs and season to taste.

SALSA VERDE

Makes 200 ml/ 1 cup
Preparation time: 15 minutes

25 g/ 1 oz/ 1 packed cup picked basil

15 g/ ¹/₂ oz/ ¹/₃ cup mint leaves

25 g/ 1 oz/ 1 cup flat leaf parsley

50 g/ 2 oz/ ¹/₄ cup capers

1 chopped garlic clove

3 anchovy fillets

25 g/ 1 oz mostarda di frutta

100 ml/ 4 fl oz/ ¹/₂ cup olive oil

Process all the ingredients and season to
taste. Mostarda di frutta are candied fruits
with a spicy mustard flavour and are
available at most Italian delicatessen.
This can keep for up to a week in
the fridge.

SAUCES

SHALLOT SAUCE

Makes 200 ml/ 7 fl oz/ ³/₄–1 cup
Preparation time: 10 minutes
Cooking time: 10 minutes

75 g/ 3 oz unsalted butter
225 g/ 8 oz shallots, finely sliced
10 sprigs thyme
150 ml/ ¹/₄ pint/ ²/₃ cup cream

Melt the butter in a saucepan before adding the shallots and thyme. Coat the shallots with the butter then cover and cook on a low heat until they are soft but not browned. Add the cream and cook for 1 minute. Remove from the heat and discard the thyme. Process the cream and shallots in a blender until smooth, sieve mixture and season generously to taste. Keep warm.

TATAKI SAUCE

Makes 375 ml/ 12¹/₂ fl oz/ 1¹/₂ cups
Preparation time: 20 minutes

75 g/ 3 oz peeled and cored apple
50 g/ 2 oz peeled carrots
25 g/ 1 oz celery
1 peeled garlic clove
50 g/ 2 oz peeled ginger
150 ml/ ¹/₄ pint/ ¹/₂ cup soy sauce
25 ml/ 1 fl oz/ ¹/₈ cup vegetable oil
50 ml/ 2 fl oz/ ¹/₄ cup toasted sesame oil
50 ml/ 2 fl oz/ ¹/₄ cup white wine vinegar
50 g/ 2 oz/ ¹/₂ cup caster sugar

Grate the apple, carrot, celery, garlic and ginger into a mixing bowl. Add the soy sauce, vegetable and sesame oils, vinegar and sugar and process with a blender. This is best made a few days before using, as it improves with age and should be strained before use.

TOFFEE SAUCE

Makes 475 ml/ 16 fl oz/ 2¹/₂ cups
Preparation time: 15 minutes
Cooking time: 10 minutes

50 g/ 2 oz unsalted butter
100 g/ 4 oz/ 1 cup demerara sugar
175 g/ 6 oz/ ¹/₂ cup golden syrup
¹/₂ vanilla pod, split lengthwise
150 ml/ ¹/₄ pint/ ²/₃ cup double cream

Put all the ingredients apart from the cream in a heavy-bottomed saucepan and stir until it comes to the boil, then reduce the heat, stirring occasionally for 10 minutes until the sugar has dissolved. Remove from the heat and mix in the cream. The sauce will keep for up to a month in the fridge and is delicious when poured over ice cream.

DRESSINGS

CHIVE OIL

Makes 100 ml/ 4 fl oz/ ¹/₂ cup
Preparation time: 5 minutes

Small bunch of chopped chives
100 ml/ 4 fl oz / ¹/₂ cup olive oil

Blend the ingredients in a bowl with a hand blender until smooth.

LEMON OIL

Makes 200 ml/ 7 fl oz/ 1 cup
Preparation time: 5 minutes

50 ml/ 2 fl oz/ ¹/₄ cup lemon juice
150 ml/ ¹/₄ pint/ ²/₃ cup extra virgin olive oil

Whisk the lemon juice and olive oil together.

LIME DRESSING

Makes 100 ml/ 4 fl oz/ ¹/₂ cup
Preparation time: 10 minutes

Zest and juice of 2 limes
1 tsp caster sugar
100 ml/ 4 fl oz/ ¹/₂ cup extra virgin olive oil

Whisk the lime juice, sugar and olive oil together and season to taste.

MOSCATEL DRESSING

Makes 4 dessert spoons
Preparation time: 1 minute

1 dessert spoon Moscatel vinegar
3 dessert spoons extra virgin olive oil

Whisk the vinegar and olive oil together.

TARRAGON DRESSING

Makes 600 ml/ 1 pint/ 2¹/₂ cups
Preparation time: 10 minutes

150 ml/ ¹/₄ pint/ ²/₃ cup vegetable oil
175 ml/ 6 fl oz/ ³/₄ cup extra virgin olive oil
3 dessert spoons chopped tarragon
1 chopped garlic clove
1 dessert spoon lemon juice
2 dessert spoons clear honey
1 tsp Dijon mustard
100 ml/ 4 fl oz/ ¹/₂ cup white wine vinegar

Mix the vegetable and olive oils together. Place the tarragon, garlic, lemon juice, honey, mustard and a pinch of salt and pepper with the white wine vinegar in a blender. Process for 30 seconds then, keeping the processor on, gradually add the oil at regular intervals until the dressing has thickened. Thin with a little water if necessary. It will last in the fridge for up to a week.

BASICS

BASIL PESTO

Makes 450 g/ 1 lb/ 2 cups
Preparation time: 20 minutes

150 g/ 5 oz/ 2¹/₂ packed cups picked basil
1 garlic clove, finely chopped
100 g/ 4 oz/ 1 packed cup grated Parmesan
100 g/ 4 oz/ 1 cup roasted and cooled pine nuts
100 ml/ 4 fl oz/ ¹/₄ cup olive oil

Put the basil, garlic, Parmesan and pine nuts into a food processor and blend, add the oil and mix until it combines with the basil paste, put in a bowl, season to taste and refrigerate until needed.

BEER BATTER

Makes 250 ml/ 8 fl oz/ 1³/₄ cups
Preparation time: 5 minutes

100 g/ 4 oz/ 1 cup self-raising flour
50 ml/ 2 fl oz/ ¹/₄ cup light beer
100 ml/ 4 fl oz/ ¹/₂ cup cold water

Whisk the flour, beer and water until smooth and refrigerate until use.

CARAMELISED ONION

Makes 450 g/ 1 lb
Preparation time: 10 minutes
Cooking time: 2 hours

2 kg/ 4¹/₂ lb sliced onions
175g/ 6 oz unsalted butter

Place the ingredients in a heavy-bottomed saucepan, cover and cook on a moderate heat for 40 minutes, stirring occasionally. Uncover and cook for 1–1¹/₂ hours on a low heat, stirring to avoid sticking to the bottom of the pan, until the juice has reduced and the onions are lightly browned.

CHICKEN STOCK

Makes 1.5 litres/ 2¹/₂ pints/ 7¹/₂ cups
Preparation time: 10 minutes
Cooking time: 3 hours

1.5 kg/ 3 lb chicken carcasses,
chopped into small pieces
4 litres/ 7 pints/ 17¹/₂ cups water
1 onion, cut in half
3 celery sticks, cut in half
3 leeks, trimmed and sliced
3 carrots, peeled and cut in half
Handful of thyme
Handful of parsley
10 peppercorns
1 bay leaf

Place the chicken carcasses and water in a large pan, bring to the boil and skim any scum from the surface, add the remaining ingredients, reduce the heat to a simmer and cook for 3 hours. Top up with water intermittently so the bones are always covered. Strain, reduce by half, season to taste and leave to cool. Any spare stock can be refrigerated or frozen.

BASICS

CHILLI JAM

Makes 450 g/ 1 lb
Preparation time: 20 minutes
Cooking time: 2 hours

450 g/ 1 lb red onions, roughly chopped

225 g/ 8 oz red peppers, deseeded and
roughly chopped

3 garlic cloves

225 g/ 8 oz quartered ripe tomatoes

25 g/ 1 oz ginger, peeled and
roughly chopped

25 g/ 1 oz coriander with roots attached

50 g/ 2 oz raisins

2 small hot red chillies

100 ml/ 4 fl oz/ ¹/₂ cup red wine vinegar

150 g/ 5 oz/ 1 cup demerara sugar

Process all the ingredients apart from the
vinegar and sugar into a pulp. Pour into a
heavy bottomed pan and add the vinegar
and sugar. When the mixture starts to
bubble, turn down the heat, cover and
cook gently for 30 minutes, stirring
occasionally. Remove the lid and cook
gently for a further 1¹/₂ hours, stirring
continuously to stop the mixture from
sticking to the bottom of the pan. It
should be thick and dark reddish-brown
in colour. Cool before refrigerating.
This keeps for 2 weeks at least.

CLARIFIED BUTTER

Makes 100 ml/ 4 fl oz/ ¹/₂ cup
Cooking time: 10 minutes

150 g/ 5 oz butter

Melt the butter in a small saucepan and
gently simmer. Skim off the white residue
that rises to the surface and discard. Pour
the clear butter into a bowl, making sure
to leave behind the milky solids at the
bottom of the saucepan.

CROUTES

Makes 4
Preparation time: 5 minutes
Cooking time: 10 minutes
Pre-heat oven to 200 °C/ 400 °F/ gas-mark 6

4 slices ciabatta bread

Olive oil

Pinch of sea salt

Place the ciabatta on an oven tray, drizzle
with olive oil and sprinkle with sea salt.
Place in the oven for 10 minutes until
golden brown, then set aside.

CUMIN CRACKERS

Makes 10
Preparation time: 5 minutes
Cooking time: 10 minutes
Pre-heat oven to 180 °C/ 350 °F/ gas-mark 4

75 g/ 3 oz/ ²/₃ cup plain flour

¹/₂ tsp baking powder

1 level dessert spoon caster sugar

1 tsp whole cumin seeds

50 ml/ 2 fl oz/ ¹/₄ cup water

25 ml/ 1 fl oz/ ¹/₈ cup olive oil

Mix the flour, baking powder, caster
sugar, a pinch of salt and pepper and
cumin seeds in a bowl and add the
water and the oil to form a sticky dough.
Knead on a floured surface for 1 minute,
divide into 10 pieces and sprinkle with
more flour before rolling each one thinly
into a long strip. Place on a baking tray
and bake for 10 minutes or until golden
brown. The crackers will keep for two
days in an airtight container.

Laurance S. Rockefeller, a well known philanthropist, pioneering venture capitalist and dedicated conservationist, auctioned property from his estate in aid of his
charity the Laurance S. Rockefeller Fund, including one of six mid-18th century Georgian silver casters, which sold for $4,200 (£2,405) in New York in 2005

BASICS

GLOBE ARTICHOKES

Makes 4
Preparation time: 15 minutes
Cooking time: 15 minutes

4 globe artichokes
Juice of 2 lemons
300 ml/ ¹/₂ pint/ 1¹/₄ cups white
wine vinegar
2 tsp salt

With a small, sharp knife, remove the
tougher, outer leaves of the artichokes
and trim the tops and the stalks. Place
them in a large saucepan, cover with
water, add the lemon juice, vinegar and
salt and weigh the artichokes down
with a plate. Cover, bring to the boil
and simmer for 15 minutes. When cool,
drain the cooking liquor and reserve.
Gently remove the remaining leaves
and scrape out the hairs, then cut into
quarters. Put into a container and pour
over the reserved cooking liquor to
stop the artichokes from discolouring.

LEMON CURD

Makes 225 ml/ 8 fl oz/ 1 cup
Preparation time: 15 minutes

100 g/ 4 oz/ 1 cup caster sugar
50 g/ 2 oz unsalted butter
Zest of 2 lemons
75 ml/ 3 fl oz/ ¹/₃ cup lemon juice
2 eggs, beaten and strained

In a heavy-bottomed pan gently heat all
of the ingredients, stirring constantly,
and without letting them boil. Take off
the heat when the mixture starts to
thicken, strain into a serving bowl and
cool. It can be kept in the fridge for up
to five days.

PARMESAN STRAWS

Makes 10
Preparation time: 30 minutes
Cooking time: 10–12 minutes
Pre-heat oven to 220 ºC/ 425 ºF/ gas-mark 7

75 g/ 3 oz puff pastry
¹/₂ tsp Dijon mustard
3 dessert spoons grated Parmesan
Pinch of cayenne pepper

Roll out pastry on a floured surface to 4
mm. (¹/₈ in.) thick and 17 by 17 cm.
(6 by 6 in.) square. Spread on mustard
and sprinkle evenly with Parmesan.
Press the cheese down, making sure it
sticks to the pastry. Sprinkle over the
cayenne pepper and cut into eight
strips. Twist each strip into a corkscrew,
keeping the cheese on the inside. Place
on a lightly greased baking tray and chill
in the fridge for 15 minutes. Cook until
risen and golden, then carefully put the
pastry on a cooling rack.

BASICS

RED ONION MARMALADE

Makes 750 g/ 1½ lb
Preparation time: 15 minutes
Cooking time: 2 hours

200 ml/ 7 fl oz/ ¾ cup red wine
200 ml/ 7 fl oz/ ¾ cup red wine vinegar
150 g/ 5 oz/ ¾ cup demerara sugar
900 g/ 2 lb red onions, finely sliced
100 g/ 4 oz unsalted butter
½ tsp salt
½ tsp pepper

In a large saucepan, heat the wine, vinegar and sugar. Add remaining ingredients, cover and cook the onions for 30 minutes until very soft, stirring occasionally. Remove the lid, turn down and cook until the liquid has evaporated, stirring more frequently so that the onions do not burn. Leave to cool before storing in the fridge.

While this amount of onions look like a lot, they reduce to a small amount when cooked and can be kept in the fridge for up to a month as a delicious accompaniment to cold meats or cheeses.

RISOTTO

Makes 450 g/ 1 lb
Preparation time: 10 minutes
Cooking time: 30 minutes

½ litre/ 17 fl oz/ 2 cups chicken stock (page 154)
1 shallot, finely chopped
1 crushed garlic clove
150 g/ 5 oz/ ¾ cup risotto rice
50 ml/ 2 fl oz/ ¼ cup white wine

Bring the chicken stock to the boil and leave to simmer. In a large pan, heat a little olive oil, add the shallot and stir until soft, then fry the garlic for 30 seconds. Add the rice and stir continuously in order to coat the grains with oil, then pour in the wine, turn up the heat and cook until absorbed. Pour in the stock, one large ladle at a time and stir, at a lower heat, until all the liquid has been absorbed. Repeat this process until all the stock has been used and the rice has a creamy consistency with a slight bite. This should take 25 minutes. Remove from the heat and set aside until needed.

VANILLA ICE CREAM

Makes 750 ml/ 1¼ pints
Preparation time: 10 minutes
Cooking time: 15 minutes
Freeze for a minimum of 2 hours

1 vanilla pod
300 ml/ ½ pint/ 1¼ cups milk
6 egg yolks
120 g/ 4½ oz/ 1 cup caster sugar
300 ml/ ½ pint/ 1¼ cups double cream

Make the ice cream mix the day before freezing, to allow the vanilla to infuse. Split the vanilla pod lengthwise, scrape out the seeds and add both the pod and seeds to the milk, simmer and remove from the heat. Whisk the egg yolks and sugar until light and fluffy, then carefully add the hot milk and mix well. Return to a clean large saucepan and stir continuously over a moderate heat, without boiling, until thickened. Pour into a bowl, add the cream, stir and cool. Sieve the mix and pour into an ice cream machine. Do not fill more than halfway as the ice cream will expand. Scoop into a container and freeze. Remove 10 minutes before serving to soften.

Marmalade ice cream: Follow the same method, adding 75 g/ 3 oz of thick-cut marmalade to the ice cream mix, after it has been cooked through.

INDEX

INDEX